ANDMASTER
FLASH

GRANDMASTER
MELLE MEL

SCORPIO

RAHIEM

KID CREOLE

BLOWFLY

DOLEMITE

TOO $HORT

RICK RUBIN

ADAM YAUCH

MR. MAGIC

BUSY BEE
STARSKI

JALIL

ECSTASY

ICE T

EAN-MICHEL
BASQUIAT

KENNY SCHARF

ZEPHYR

DONDI

HENRY
CHALFANT

JDL

EASY AD

ALMIGHTY KG

ZULU NATION

MC DJ FLAVOR

HIP HOP FAMILY TREE

ED PISKOR

FANTAGRAPHICS BOOKS INC

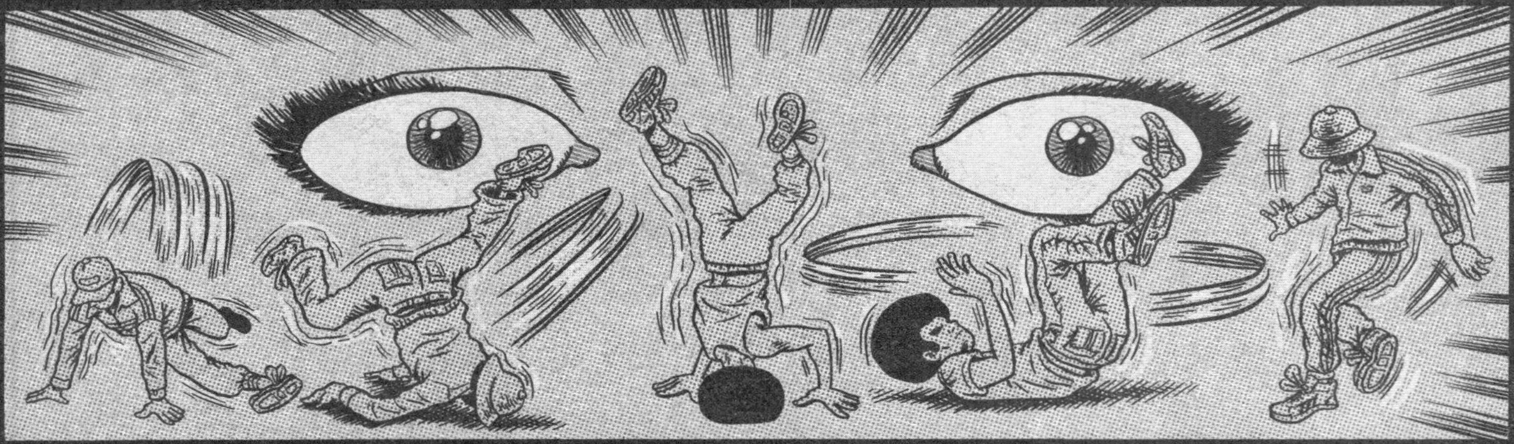

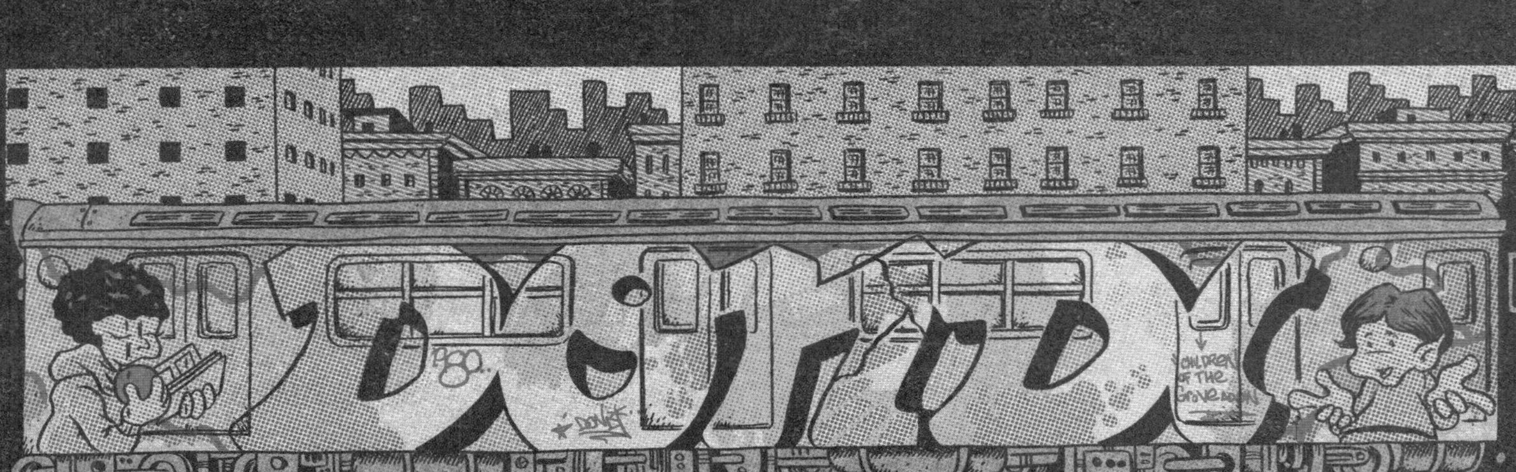
CHILDREN OF THE

FANTAGRAPHICS TREASURY EDITION

HIP HOP FAMILY TREE

TABLE OF CONTENTS

"NO MATTER HOW HARD YOU TRY YOU CAN'T STOP US NOW."

AFRIKA BAMBAATAA
AND THE SOULSONIC FORCE
RENEGADES OF FUNK, 1983

INTRODUCTION
BY
CHARLIE AHEARN

I RECOGNIZED A FELLOW TRAVELER ON THE HIP HOP ORIGINS TIP THE MOMENT I SAW ED'S **HIP HOP FAMILY TREE** (ONLINE **BRAINROT** SAMPLER PAGES). HERE WERE THE EARLY OBSCURE DETAILS I PRIZED, LIKE MY FAV MC, BEFORE HE CHANGED HIS NAME, POPPED A RHYME AND CHANGED THE GAME. WHO? **ED** IS HIGH ON **COKE LA ROCK, EDDIE CHEBA** AND **KURTIS BLOW**, AND LOTS OF PIONEERS YOU NEVER HEARD ABOUT 'CAUSE ED'S MISSION IS THAT VAST—TAKING US WAY, WAY BACK.

NOW WE GOT #2, TRACING STUFF LIKE **ED'S** "FLASHBACK TO 1979" WHEN "**FLASH IS ON THE BEAT BOX**" BECAME THE MELODIC STREET HOOK WHEN IT WAS RECORDED ON A **ZULU JAM** CASSETTE THEN HAWKED ALL OVER THE **BRONX**. THREE YEARS LATER A BOOTLEG LP OFF THAT CASSETTE REACHES **SYLVIA ROBINSON** AT **SUGAR HILL** AND SHE DESPERATELY RUSHES **FLASH** AND THE FURIOUS INTO A STUDIO VERSION THAT "BOILS THE HEART AND SOUL OUT OF THE ORIGINAL." **ED** LIKES THE RAW, ORIGINAL VERSION.

ED HAS DONE HIS HOMEWORK WITH STORIES SO DENSE I HAD TO PAUSE AFTER EACH PAGE. **ED'S** ARTWORK BLEEDS OLD SCHOOL COMICS, **MARVEL**OUS GRAPHICS AND HE EVEN GOT THE TEXTURE RIGHT. HE LIKES FUNKY CARICATURES (CHECK HIS **MELLE MEL, RUSSELL SIMMONS** OR **KOOL MOE DEE**!) AND TWISTS OF FATE, LIKE HOW UNKNOWN GUITARIST **JERRY LORDAN'S** "**APACHE**", BECAME A **UK** HIT, WAS COVERED BY THE **INCREDIBLE BONGO BAND** AND ONLY LATER DUBBED THE **BBOY** ANTHEM BY **HERC**.

LAST SUMMER **PISKOR** MADE A TWENTY-FOUR HOUR **WILD STYLE** PILGRIMAGE FROM HIS **PITTSBURGH** TO THE **LES NYC** JUST AS **BUSY BEE** TOOK THE STAGE AT THE AMPHITHEATER. **ED** BROUGHT A LITTLE SECRET EDITION **WILD STYLE** COMIC GIVEN OUT TO A FEW LUCKY FANS OF THE MOVIE. I WAS BACKSTAGE CHASING TALENT AND I DIDN'T GET TO SPEAK WITH **ED** UNTIL AFTER VOL 1 DROPPED INTO MY MAILBOX.

ED TOLD ME HOW HEARING THE **WILD STYLE** DVD COMMENTARY WITH ME AND **FAB 5** SPARKED HIS OBSESSION WITH HIP HOP'S ORIGINS, ESPECIALLY **FRED'S** CHALLENGE TO RE-DISCOVER EARLY CLASSICS LIKE **FUNKY FOUR'S ENJOY** MASTERPIECE **RAPPIN' AND ROCKIN' THE HOUSE**. HEARING THESE RECORDS SET OFF VIVID CARTOONS IN HIS CORTEX WHICH HE COULDN'T DESCRIBE. ED JUST **HAD TO DRAW THEM.**

MIND YOU, IT TAKES DAYS FOR HIM TO COMPLETE A PAGE WITH FIVE OR SIX PANELS. THIS LARGE FORMAT LABOR OF LOVE YOU HOLD IN YOUR HAND HARKENS BACK TO A **DC** CLASSIC FROM THE MID-'70S, **SUPERMAN VS. MUHAMMAD ALI**, ISSUED IN A LARGE FORMAT AND STILL TREASURED DURING **ED'S** TEEN YEARS. KEEP IN MIND **ED** WASN'T EVEN BORN UNTIL 1982, THE SAME YEAR **WILD STYLE** FIRST HIT THE BIG SCREEN. BUT THE KEY INFLUENCE TO

ED'S APPROACH WAS THE **MARVEL** MASTER **JACK KIRBY**, WHO CREATED MUCH OF THE ARTISTRY UNDER THAT BANNER, SEEN MOST PROVOCATIVELY IN **THE BLACK PANTHER** BOOKS WHICH VISUALIZED ACTION PANELS OF PEOPLE OF COLOR AND THEIR LIFE EXPERIENCES.

I WILL ADMIT IT **IS** SHOCKING AT FIRST TO SEE ONESELF AS A COMIC BOOK CHARACTER. I WON'T QUIBBLE WITH THE NOSE, BUT HE DID GET SOME COOL NERDY DETAILS IN THERE, LIKE ME HOLDING A CLIPBOARD WHILE DIRECTING **WILD STYLE** (TRUE) ALTHOUGH I DELIGHTED TO SEE ME IN **NIVA'S** BEDROOM SCENE HOLDING WHAT LOOKS LIKE A **CANON SCOOPIC** (**CLIVE DAVISON** ACTUALLY SHOT THE SCENE) WITH MY TONGUE OUT IN DEEP CONCENTRATION. THAT'S COMIX!

THE **A TO THE K** STICK-UP SCENE INSPIRED SOME GRITTY ACTION PANELS FROM **ED**, COMBINING SCENE QUOTES, COMMENTARIES AND A NOTE: **SAWED OFF** IN A SQUARE YELLOW BOX WITH ARROW TO **POOKIE'S** PIECE. **ED** VISUALIZED THE **STOOP RAP** WITH US ENJOYING **RODNEY'S MOM'S** HOSPITALITY WITH **FRED** ON THE POT READING A **LIFE** MAGAZINE (POETIC LICENSE?) I APPRECIATE LITTLE BITS OF REAL-LIFE INFO, LIKE IN THE AMPHITHEATER SCENE WHERE **BUSY BEE'S** GOT THE WHOLE PLACE CLAPPING THE HELL OUT OF THAT SERIAL KILLER AND **ED** FOOTNOTES THAT **WAYNE WILLIAMS** WAS ALL OVER THE NEWS (BUT WAS AS YET STILL UNIDENTIFIED). I LOVED THE ACTION PANEL OF **FROSTY FREEZE** (RIP) IN MID-SUICIDE MOVE WITH SPEED LINES!

THIS BOOK IS BOUND TO START BEEF, WHAT WITH ALL THESE MC'S, EVERYBODY'S GOT THEIR OWN VERSION. NO, THE **NEGRIL** WAS NOT A VAST CLUB WITH DISCO BALLS, BUT I DID LOVE THE NOIRISH ACTION SCENE OF US BEING CHASED IN THE YARD WITH THE **ZDF** PRODUCER, EVEN THOUGH IT WAS DAYTIME. BUT DAMN, THIS BOOK IS SUCH A BLAST TO READ! **YES, YES, Y'ALL** AND MAY IT INSPIRE AS MANY QUESTIONS AS IT ANSWERS.

— **CHARLIE AHEARN, 2014**
FILM DIRECTOR, **WILD STYLE**

THIS IS DEDICATED TO ALLLLLL YOU BITCHES!

FANTAGRAPHICS BOOKS

7563 LAKE CITY WAY NE
SEATTLE, WASHINGTON 98115

EDITORIAL LIAISON: GARY GROTH
COPY EDITING ASSISTANCE: JANICE LEE
PRODUCTION: PAUL BARESH
DESIGN CONSULTATION: EMORY LIU
PUBLISHER: GARY GROTH
ASSOCIATE PUBLISHER: ERIC REYNOLDS

HIP HOP FAMILY TREE BOOK 2: 1975-1983 (VOL 2.)

THIRD FANTAGRAPHICS BOOKS EDITION: JULY 2017

ISBN 978-1-60699-756-7

PRINTED IN CHINA

FANTAGRAPHICS WOULD LIKE TO THANK: RANDALL BETHUNE • BIG PLANET COMICS • BLACK HOOK PRESS, JAPAN • NICK CAPETILLO •
KEVIN CZAPIEWSKI • JOHN DIBELLO • JUAN MANUEL DOMINGUEZ • MATHIEU DOUBLET • DAN EVANS III • THOMAS EYKEMANS • SCOTT
FRITSCH-HAMMES • COCO AND EDDIE GORODETSKY • KAREN GREEN • TED HAYCRAFT • EDUARDO TAKEO "LIZARKEO" IGARASHI •
NEVDON JAMGOCHIAN • ANDY KOOPMANS • PHILIP NEL • VANESSA PALACIOS • KURT SAYENGA • ANNE LISE ROSTGAARD SCHMIDT •
CHRISTIAN SCHREMSER • SECRET HEADQUARTERS • PAUL VAN DIJKEN • MUNGO VAN KRIMPEN-HALL • JASON AARON WONG • THOMAS
ZIMMERMANN

IN **1981** AS THE BASIC STRUCTURE OF **RAP MUSIC** BEGINS TO CRYSTALLIZE, A CERTAIN BARRIER TO ENTRY FORMS FOR YOUNGER KIDS WHO **CAN'T** REALLY AFFORD **MASSIVE** COLLECTIONS OF RECORDS, TURNTABLES, AND SOUND EQUIPMENT.

IN THE TRUE SPIRIT OF THE CULTURE, THOUGH, **WORK-AROUNDS** DEVELOP TO BREAK DOWN SUCH OBSTACLES. **MOST** KIDS WILL BANG BEATS ON A DESKTOP, BUT THIS DUDE IS **DIFFERENT**.

BOOM CLICK C-CLICK OOMP BOOM!

DO **TOYS IN THE ATTIC,** NEX'!

BOOM DAP BOOM BOOM BOOM DAP

THE **NOVELTY** OF **DOUGLAS E. DAVIS'S** PERCUSSIVE "**BEATBOXING**" QUICKLY DISARMS OPPONENTS, MAKING HIM A RAP BATTLE **MASTER.** INSPIRED TO MOVE A STEP FURTHER, HE DECIDES TO DEMONSTRATE HIS **UNIQUE** ABILITY TO **BOBBY ROBINSON,** THE OWNER OF THE RAP MUSIC LABEL **ENJOY RECORDS** AND THE PROPRIETOR OF **BOBBY'S HAPPY HOUSE RECORDS** STORE.

HE'S GOOD.

THE BOY IS GOOD!

BOOM BOMP BA-CLICK OOMP!

LEAVING **NOTHING** TO CHANCE, BOBBY'S NEPHEW AND CURRENT SUGAR HILL RECORDING ARTIST, **SPOONIE GEE,** LIVES ACROSS THE STREET FROM THE YOUNG PERFORMER.

SPOONIE! **YO, SPOONIE GEE!** PEEP OUT THIS GOOD SHIT! I'M TRYNA GET ON **REKKIDS**!

SAY WHA?

HA HA!!

ZIGGA BA-BA BOMP

HA HA! OH MAN, I KNOW YOU! THERE'S **ALWAYS** A CROWD AROUND YOU. WHAT YOU SAY YOUR NAME WAS?

DOUG E. FRESH!

7

ALONZO BROWN, AKA LONNIE LOVE, AKA **MR. HYDE**, APPRECIATED HIS FEW CHANCES TO RAP ON WAX, BUT IN AN ACT OF **PRAGMATISM**, DECIDES IT'S A GOOD TIME TO JOIN THE **AIR FORCE**.

SO, **BABY**, YOU KNOW I'M SHIPPIN' OUT SOON, **RIGHT**?

THE NEARLY BANKRUPT **PROFILE RECORDS** LABEL, HOWEVER, IS UNWILLING TO CASH IN THEIR CHIPS. DOWN TO THEIR LAST PENNIES AND LOOKING TO MAKE ONE LAST RECORD, THEY CALL THE **ONE** RAPPER THEY KNOW.

I'M DOWN, I GUESS. **ON ONE CONDITION...**

THE LABEL SPENDS **MOST** OF THEIR MONEY IN ACQUIRING THE RIGHTS TO USE TOM TOM CLUB'S **GENIUS OF LOVE** AS THE INSTRUMENTAL FOR THE NEW RECORD. SOME MORE MONEY GOES TO **JOE TUCCI** TO REINTERPRET THE TRACK WITH A HIP HOP FLAIR.

THE LINN, LM-1 DRUM MACHINE

MR. HYDE INSISTS THAT HIS PARTNER, **DR. JECKYLL**, JOINS HIM TO RECORD **GENIUS RAP**, AND THEY LAUNCH INTO 7 MINUTES' WORTH OF THEIR **TRIED** AND **TRUE** ROUTINES.

WE WALK ON WATER AND FLY THROUGH **AIR**...

...GOT PITCHERS OF MYSELF ON MUH **UNDERWEAR**...

GARAGE STUDIO

WITHIN A DAY OR TWO, A REEL-TO-REEL TAPE OF GENIUS RAP IS SENT TO **MR. MAGIC** AT WHBI 105.9 FM.

...LIKE GINGER ROGERS AND FREDDY ASTAIRE...

LIKE BOO-BOO, GIRL, AND **YOGI THE BEAR**...

24 HOURS AFTER THE INITIAL RADIO PLAY, THE BOYS AT PROFILE, **CORY ROBBINS** AND **STEVE PLOTNICKI**, HEAD TO A FEW RECORD SHOPS TO GAUGE ANY RESPONSE TO THE TRACK.

YOU MIGHT BE THE 20TH KIDS TODAY ASKIN' FOR THAT REKKID.

A WHOPPING SUCCESS FOR THE SINKING LABEL, **GENIUS RAP** SELLS 150,000 RECORDS RAPIDLY, GIVING PROFILE **6 FIGURES**' WORTH OF PROFITS. WITH THIS FIRM POSITION, THE LABEL SIGNS DR. JECKYLL AND MR. HYDE TO A DEAL FOR MORE RECORDS.

$2000 TO PUBLISH ALL YOUR NEW MUSIC FOR PROFILE... HOW'S THAT SOUND?

MR. HYDE **MASTERFULLY** TRAVERSES THE LAST OBSTACLE BETWEEN **HIMSELF** AND HIS NEW-FOUND **RECORDING CAREER**.

NO SIR. I'M NOT GONNA BE ABLE TO PARTICIPATE IN THE AIR FORCE LIKE I WANTED TO...

...MY MOTHER... >sob< SHE GOT A **BRAIN TUMOR**...

GENIUS RAP ISN'T THE ONLY SONG TO USE THE CATCHY BREAK FROM TOM TOM CLUB'S GENIUS OF LOVE. SUGAR HILL RECORDS PRODUCED A NEW 12-INCH BY GRANDMASTER FLASH AND THE FURIOUS FIVE CALLED IT'S NASTY, USING CHRIS FRANTZ AND TINA WEYMOUTH'S POPULAR RIFF.

WE ADVERTISE...

...AND SPECIALIZE...

...IN THE EXERCISE AND WE'LL ENERGIZE...

...THE YOUNG LADIES' THIGHS...

...CAUSE ALL THE FLY GUYS...

...NATURES TO RISE RIGHT BEFORE YOUR EYES!!

BACKSTAGE ONE NIGHT, AFTER FLASH AND THE FURIOUS PERFORM THE SONG, PITTSBURGH PIRATES GREAT **WILLIE STARGELL** CONFRONTS THE GROUP.

Y'ALL SHOULD BE ASHAMED OF YUH SELFS!

Y'ALL ARE NASTY! UP ON STAGE LIKE THAT GRABBIN' ON YUH SELF'S!

...IN FRONT OF MY DAUGHTERS!

AW YEAH?! WELL IF YOU PAID MORE ATTENTION TO YA KIDS, YOU MIGHT KNOW SOMETHIN' ABOUT US...

...AN' LET ME TELL YOU SOMETHIN', POPS!

WE NASTY!

HA HA!

IN 1960, **JERRY LORDAN** CREATED A CATCHY GUITAR RIFF CALLED **APACHE**, INSPIRED BY THE 1954 BURT LANCASTER MOVIE OF THE SAME NAME.

MONTHS LATER, WHILE ON TOUR WITH THE ENGLISH BAND **THE SHADOWS**, LORDAN SHARED THE SONG WITH THEM, THINKING IT FIT THEIR STYLE. HE WAS **RIGHT**, THEY RECORDED THE SONG, AND IT PEAKED AT NO. **1** ON THE BRITISH CHARTS.

APACHE DIDN'T REALLY RESONATE IN THE U.S., WHICH MIGHT HAVE ADDED TO THE REASON WHY **MICHAEL VINER'S INCREDIBLE BONGO BAND** DECIDED TO CREATE THEIR **OWN** VERSION OF THE TUNE IN 1973. THEIR RECORD DIDN'T SHARE THE SAME FATE AS **THE SHADOWS**...

THANKFULLY, **DJ KOOL HERC** DISCOVERS THE BONGO BAND JOINT A FEW YEARS LATER!

A **HIT** AT HIP HOP JAMS, APACHE BECOMES AN IMPORTANT WEAPON IN **MOST** DJ ARSENALS, RENDERING THE RECORD A BIT EXPENSIVE AND/OR HARD TO FIND. IN 1980 **PAUL WINLEY** DID LATE DJ'S A FAVOR BY INCLUDING **APACHE** ON THE THIRD VOLUME OF HIS BOOTLEG, BREAK-BEAT COMPILATION SERIES, **SUPER DISCO BRAKES**.

APACHE IS ONE OF THE MAIN INGREDIENTS SAMPLED ON **ADVENTURES OF GRANDMASTER FLASH ON THE WHEELS OF STEEL**, SOLIDIFYING THE INSTRUMENTAL'S MANTLE AS BEING AN IMPORTANT, BACKBONE BREAK IN HIP HOP.

IN 1981, SUGAR HILL RECORDS FINDS SOME SUCCESS PRODUCING A **RAP** VERSION OF APACHE USING THEIR FLAGSHIP ARTISTS, **THE SUGARHILL GANG**.

JUMP ON IT!!!

ACROSS THE COUNTRY, **RAP** RECORDS ARE REALLY BEGINNING TO PROLIFERATE. FOR **FANS** OF THE **MUSIC** WHO ARE FAR REMOVED FROM THE **HIP HOP** SCENE OF THE **SOUTH BRONX**, COMPARISONS ARE DRAWN TO MORE **FAMILIAR** SOURCES INCLUDING **PARTY RECORDS**, WHICH ARE FULL OF CRASS **RHYMING**, COMEDY, AND PARODY.

BLOWFLY

SHITTIN' OFF THE DOCK OF THE BAY! WATCHIN' MY GREAT BIG TURDS FLOAT AWAY!

RUDY RAY MOORE

...AND THE CRABS WAS MADDER THAN A **MUTHAFUCKA**...

...TO SEE THAT DOLEMITE ATE 'EM OUTTA THEY GOD-DAMN **SUPPAH**!

YOU **CRAZY**, MAN!

IN **OAKLAND, CALIFORNIA**, 15-YEAR-OLD TODD ANTHONY SHAW, AKA **TOO SHORT**, CLEARLY SEES THESE **PARALLELS** ONCE THE **RECORDS** HIT HIS NEIGHBORHOOD.

SPOONIE GEE IS THE **ONLY** PLAYER IN THE GAME. HE LIKE **GOLDIE** IN **THE MACK**.

TOO SHORT HAS A **REPUTATION** FOR BEING THE **BEST** RAPPER AT SCHOOL, AND HIS PAL **FREDDY B** IS INTERESTED IN **MONETIZING** THEIR TALENT.

THIS **GENIUS** RAP GOT SUCH A FLY BEAT TO IT...

...WHAT IF WE **RAP** OVER TOP OF THE INSTRUMENTAL? WE COULD MAKE SOME TAPES AND SELL 'EM.

!

WE CAN GIVE IT A TRY...

...BUT WHO THE **FUCK** IS GONNA HAVE **MONEY** TO BUY OUR SHIT?

DRUG DEALERS!

HA HA! WORD!

RICK RUBIN'S KNOWLEDGE OF RAP MUSIC AND ROCK AND ROLL DEEPENED. HE IS QUOTED IN HIS YEARBOOK: "I WANNA PLAY LOUD, I WANT TO BE HEARD, I WANT ALL TO KNOW I'M NOT ONE OF THE HERD."

LINES FORM ON MY FACE AND HANDS. LINES FORM FROM THE UPS AND DOWNS...

..I'M IN THE MIDDLE, WITHOUT ANY PLANS. I'M A BOY AND I'M A MAN...

STRATEGICALLY ENROLLING AT NYU, RICK CAN TRAVEL EASILY TO HIP HOP VENUES LIKE HARLEM WORLD, WHERE LOVEBUG STARSKI IS RELEASING HIS FIRST SINGLE, POSITIVE LIFE.

RAP RECORDS AREN'T ANYTHING LIKE THESE LIVE SHOWS...

HE EVEN SNEAKS HIS WAY INTO THE DISCO FEVER AROUND THE TIME THE VENUE'S HOUSE EMCEE, SWEET G, RECORDS A HEARTBEAT RAP.

IF THEY'D ONLY TRANSLATE THIS ENERGY ON WAX ...

RICK RUBIN IS ALWAYS KEEPING HIS FOOT IN THE PUNK ROCK WORLD. HIS NYU DORM ISN'T FAR FROM THE ENERGETIC BANDS PLAYING CLUBS LIKE C.B.G.B, AND MAX'S KANSAS CITY.

BAD BRAINS

DEAD KENNEDYS

THE MISFITS

HENRY...

A COMMON THREAD BETWEEN THE THREE ABOVE-MENTIONED BANDS IS THAT THE SAME GROUP OF OBNOXIOUS TEENAGERS OPENED UP SHOWS FOR THEM.

ADAM YAUCH

B-E-A-S-T-I-E!

KATE SCHELLENBACH

MICHAEL DIAMOND

JOHN BERRY

AS NEW **HIT** SONGS INVADE THE MINDS OF THE **MASSES**, IT'S AN **EASY** BET THAT THEY'LL END UP BEING, QUITE LITERALLY, **INSTRUMENTAL** INSPIRATION FOR RAP RECORDS. THIS HOLDS **TRUE** FOR TAANA GARDNER'S **HEARTBEAT**, WHICH YIELDS A **GANG** OF RAP SINGLES.

ANOTHER "HEARTBEAT" RIFF IS THE **DEBUT** 12-INCH BY **T SKI VALLEY** CALLED **CATCH THE BEAT.**

SO... ...SWEET!

HE'S BEEN A FIXTURE IN THE **HIP HOP** WORLD FOR YEARS, WORKING WITH DJ'S LIKE **KOOL HERC** AND **AJ**, AND WARMING UP FOR EMCEE'S LIKE **CHIEF-ROCKER BUSY BEE.**

T, YOU COULDA BEEN ON REKKIDS IF YOU'DA STUCK WIF US.*

* RAPPIN' ALL OVER BY THE YOUNGER GENERATION. HHFT#1

BY DAY, T SKI VALLEY WORKS AT **BRAD'S RECORD AUDIO DEN.**

YOU BES' GET HIP TO THIS RAP STUFF, MAN!

RAP IS RULIN'!

BRAD, LIKE **BOBBY ROBINSON**, ALSO OWNS AND OPERATES A RECORD LABEL. **CLOCK TOWER** PUTS OUT **REGGAE** RECORDS MOSTLY.

IN FACT, **WE** SHOULD BE MAKIN' SOME RAP RECORDS, BRAD, MAN!

AFTER CRUNCHING SOME NUMBERS AND SEEING HOW POPULAR RAP MUSIC IS BECOMING, BRAD DECIDES TO **INVEST** IN A T SKI VALLEY RECORD.

THE COKE MACHINE AT THIS RECORDING STUDIO IS FULL OF **COLT 45!**

PROMOTING CATCH THE BEAT BECOMES A BIT OF AN OBSTACLE SINCE **RADIO** DJ **MR. MAGIC** IS **NOT** INTO THE JOINT.

...NO NEED FOR **ANOTHER** HEART-BEAT RECORD...

AS A **PLAN B**, BRAD PAYS FOR AIRTIME ON MAGIC'S PROGRAM TO RUN A **COMMERCIAL** FOR THE AUDIO DEN RECORD SHOP. T SKI VALLEY'S SINGLE PLAYS **UNDERNEATH** THE STRATEGIC ADVERTISEMENT.

IT'S THE G-R-A THE "N", THE "D", THE G-R-O THE "V" THE "E"

JALIL, MR. MAGIC'S **INTERN**, BEGINS FIELDING CALL AFTER CALL FROM PEOPLE **CURIOUS** ABOUT THE MYSTERIOUS SONG IN THE BACKGROUND.

33 CALLS SO FAR TODAY, MAGIC.

BY POPULAR DEMAND! T SKI VALLEY'S **CATCH THE BEAT!**

MAN, I WAS **BLITZED!** WHY DIDN'T NO ONE CATCH THAT I SPELLED "**GRAND GROOVE**" WRONG?

* GRAND GROOVE IS THE RECORD LABEL CREATED FOR THE RELEASE OF T SKI VALLEY'S SINGLE.

JUST A FEW WEEKS AGO, **TRACY MARROW** DISCOVERED THAT HE COULD GET AN **HONORABLE DISCHARGE** FROM THE **ARMY** SINCE HE IS THE MAIN FINANCIAL SUPPORT FOR HIS DAUGHTER.

YES, MA'AM, I NEED TO GIT MY WATCH CLEANED.

WHILE STATIONED IN **HAWAII**, HE WAS ABLE TO PURCHASE TOP QUALITY EQUIPMENT IN PREPARATION FOR BECOMING A **MOBILE DJ** TO MAKE MONEY IN **CIVILIAN** LIFE.

PRETTY QUICKLY, HE FELT THE TASK OF **LUGGING** AROUND ALL THAT EQUIPMENT WASN'T WORTH THE **PENNIES** THAT HE MADE AT PARTIES.

MY SON CLEANS EVERYTHING IN THE BACK ROOM. IT'LL ONLY TAKE A FEW MINUTES.

...BE RIGHT BACK.

TRUTHFULLY, HE'S BECOME MORE INTERESTED IN **RHYMING** ON THE **MIC**, ANYHOW.

YO, **EVIL**! IS IT A **BET**?

SHE'S OUTTA SIGHT, HOMES...

BEING IN **LOS ANGELES**, FAR REMOVED FROM THE RAP MUSIC LABELS ON THE **EAST COAST**, TRACY CAN'T BEGIN TO **IMAGINE** HE COULD MAKE **ANY** MONEY RAPPING.

..IT'S..

...A BET!

RIP AND RUN!!

HE **DAMN SURE** KNOWS HE WON'T FIND ANY KIND OF WORK AS LUCRATIVE AS PULLING "**LICKS**". ONCE HE **FENCES** THESE WRIST WATCHES, HE'LL HAVE EARNED $25,000.

HA HA!

IN HIS DOWNTIME, TRACY ENTERTAINS HIS FRIENDS BY RECITING QUOTES FROM **ICEBERG SLIM** NOVELS AND "**CRIP RAPPING**" HIS OWN **STYLE** OF RHYMES.

SO WE FELL TO THE GROUND, AIMING FOR HIS **HEAD**. ONE MORE SHOT, NIGGA WAS **DEAD**. WALKED OVER TO HIM, TOOK HIS **GUN**, SPIT IN HIS FACE AND BEGAN TO **RUN**!

YOU COOL LIKE **ICE, T**.

IN A POST-**RAPTURE*** WORLD, **FAB FIVE FREDDY** IS ONE STEP CLOSER TO HIS **MAJOR** GOAL...

I'M CURATING AN ART SHOW AT THE **MUDD** CLUB...

* THE HIT SONG BY **BLONDIE**.

...I'M CALLING IT "**BEYOND WORDS: GRAFFITI BASED, ROOTED, INSPIRED WORKS.**" THIS IS GONNA BE A PERFECT OPPORTUNITY TO MIX THE **UPTOWN** HIP HOP SCENE WITH THE **DOWNTOWN** ART WORLD!

TSSSSSS

FRED'S GRAFF COLLABORATOR, **FUTURA 2000**, AND HIS WALL STREET CREDIT ANALYST/ART DEALER PAL, **MICHAEL HOLMAN**, HELP VET TALENT FOR THE UPCOMING EVENT.

I'LL START MAKIN' SOME PHONECALLS.

BEDFORD STUYVESANT

TSSSSSSS

THE ARTISTS IN THE PROGRAM ARE CHOSEN BECAUSE THEIR WORK DRAWS **DIRECTLY** FROM GRAFFITI AND URBAN ART.

| KEITH HARING | RAMMELLZEE | JEAN-MICHEL BASQUIAT | KENNY SCHARF |
| ZEPHYR | DONDI WHITE | HENRY CHALFANT, MARTHA COOPER | IGGY POP |

AFRIKA BAMBAATAA AND **DJ JAZZY JAY** SPIN THE RECORDS FOR THE OPENING.

THE PINK PANTHER SONG?

TO ROUND OUT THE ENTERTAINMENT, SEVERAL GROUPS OF EMCEES COME THROUGH TO DROP SOME OF THEIR FINEST ROUTINES. AMONG THEM ARE **CHIEFROCKER BUSY BEE**, THE FANTASTIC 5, AND **THE COLD CRUSH BROTHERS**...

IT WAS A LONG TIME AGO, BUT I'LL NEVER **FORGET**. I GOT CAUGHT IN THE BED WITH A GIRL NAMED **YVETTE**.

WELL, I WAS SCARED LIKE HELL, BUT I STILL GOT **AWAY**. THAT'S WHY I'M HERE TELLIN' YOU **TODAY**...

...WELL I WAS TEARIN' SHIT UP 'TIL 'BOUT A QUARTER TO **THREE**...

...SHE SAID "CAZ, SOMEBODY'S COMIN'!" I SAID, "YEAH, ME!"

LEO CASTELLI, THE ART DEALER WHO REPRESENTS **WARHOL**, **LICHTENSTEIN**, AND **FRANK STELLA**, TO NAME-DROP A FEW, IS ASKED ABOUT HIS THOUGHTS ON THE **BEYOND WORDS** SHOW.

I THINK THEY ARE PRODUCING SOME OF THE **BEST** WORK BY YOUNG ARTISTS TODAY.

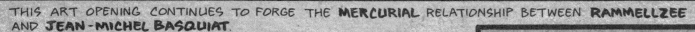

THIS ART OPENING CONTINUES TO FORGE THE **MERCURIAL** RELATIONSHIP BETWEEN **RAMMELLZEE** AND **JEAN-MICHEL BASQUIAT.**

YOU MEAN TO TELL ME YO' DADDY OWNED THE **ENTIRE** BUILDING WHERE YOU GREW UP? AND YOU **CHOOSE** TO LOOK LIKE A **FUCKIN'** BUM?

YOU GOT A **RESPONSIBILITY** TO YUH BRUTHAS TO REPRESENT US BETTER, MAN!

RAMM BRINGS BASQUIAT TO A MEETING OF THE FIVE PERCENT NATION OF ISLAM.

...SO, ABOUT THOSE **BEAN PIES** I HEAR SO MUCH ABOUT?

I'D SAY THAT SHOW WAS AS GOOD AS IT COULD HAVE BEEN, MAN.

THIS LETS US **KNOW** THAT THE DOWNTOWN SCENE MIGHT **REALLY** BE READY FOR **HIP HOP.**

I THINK THIS DUDE, **MALCOLM McLAREN** MIGHT HAVE A FEW IDEAS ABOUT WHAT WE CAN DO NEXT.

MALCOLM WHO?

DON'T SWEAT IT, FRED. I GOT THIS ONE!

DEEP IN THE BRONX RIVER HOUSING PROJECTS...

HEY!

IT'S GREAT, RIGHT, MALCOLM?

THIS MIGHT BE THE GREATEST CULTURAL DISCOVERY OF THE 20TH CENTURY...

CAN WE GO NOW, MICHAEL?

SEEING **ALL** THAT HE NEEDED TO, **MALCOLM MCLAREN** MAKES A FEW MOVES TO BRING **HIP HOP** INTO A MORE COMFORTABLE SETTING IN TOWN.

...AND THESE **KIDS** SPIN ON THEIR **HEADS**!

RUZA BLUE, THE MANAGER OF MCLAREN'S POSH NEW YORK BOUTIQUE, **DOESN'T** NEED THE HARD SELL, BUT SHE LISTENS **ANYWAY**.

...AND THAT **MESS** WRITTEN ON ALL THE **SUBWAY CARS** FACTORS INTO THIS, SOMEHOW...

...BUT, THE REAL **STARS** OF THE SHOW ARE THESE BOYS WHO **OBLITERATE** THEIR MOTHER'S RECORD COLLECTION...

ON SEPTEMBER 14, 1981, THE CROWD IS IN FOR A **SURPRISE** WHEN THEY SEE THE **OPENING** ACT FOR MCLAREN'S POP/PUNK BAND **BOW WOW WOW** AT THE **RITZ**. ALL **FOUR** ROOT ELEMENTS OF HIP HOP ON **DISPLAY**, AT THE SAME TIME, WHETHER TICKET HOLDERS ARE **READY** FOR IT OR NOT.

JAZZY JAY

AFRIKA BAMBAATAA

FUTURA 2000

ROCK STEADY CREW

...BORN AND RAISED ON THE PLANET **MARS**, I USED TO CHILL AND ROCK WITH THE **STARS**...

FAB FIVE FREDDY

...TIL ONE DAY I DECIDED TO **SPLIT**! I WENT TO EARTH ON A ROCKET **SHIP**...

AT THE END OF THE SHOW, **DJ JAZZY JAY** CAN'T **HELP** BUT OBSERVE...

THERE WAS WHITE FOLKS THERE WITH **PURPLE HAIR**, MAN!

MICHAEL HOLMAN IS PLENTY SATISFIED WITH THE EVENT WHEN APPROACHED BY **RUZA BLUE**, WHO, LIKE JAZZY JAY, CAN'T **BELIEVE** HER EYES.

I **KNOW** A PLACE IN TOWN WHERE WE MIGHT BE ABLE TO DO THIS **EVERY** WEEK!

WORD?

THE RESULTING PARTNERSHIP BETWEEN **MICHAEL HOLMAN** AND **RUZA"KOOL LADY"BLUE** YIELDS A **WEEKLY** HIP HOP PARTY AT THE REGGAE NIGHTCLUB **NEGRIL**, IN THE HEART OF MONEY-MAKING MANHATTAN.

DEFYING MAX. OCCUPANCY/FIRE CODES, THE EVENT HAS TO MOVE TO A BIGGER VENUE TO SURVIVE. THE CHELSEA-BASED ROLLER DISCO **ROXY** BECOMES HOME TO THE WEEKLY "**WHEELS OF STEEL**" PARTIES. ONE CRUCIAL NIGHT ESTABLISHES THE UNIFIED VIBE BETWEEN **UPTOWN** AND **DOWNTOWN** WHEN THE ROXY SCREENS THE **SEX PISTOLS** FILM, **THE GREAT ROCK'N'ROLL SWINDLE**, FOLLOWED BY A DJ SET BY **JAZZY JAY** AND **AFRIKA BAMBAATAA**. EVERYBODY HANGS AT THE ROXY, THOUGH THEY DON'T **ALL** KNOW EACH OTHER... **YET**...

MALCOLM McLAREN'S INTEREST HASN'T WAVERED SINCE FIRST BEING EXPOSED TO THIS NEW **CULTURE**.

...**FAB FIVE FREDDY**, MEET MALCOLM McLAREN...

THANK YOU, **RUZA**. HAVE YOU EVER THOUGHT ABOUT MAKING A RECORD?

MALCOLM'S REPUTATION PRECEDES HIM WHEN **FREDDY** ASKS HIS FRIENDS FOR ADVICE. PALS LIKE **DEBBIE HARRY** AND **CHRIS STEIN**...

HMMM... I'M NOT SO SURE ABOUT THIS, FREDDY...

... AND **THE CLASH**...

...HE'S A **FUCKA**!

FAB FIVE FREDDY ENDS UP INTRODUCING **McLAREN** TO **JUST ALLAH** AND **C DIVINE, THE WORLD FAMOUS SUPREME TEAM**, A PAIR OF RADIO DJ'S WHO HAVE AIRTIME **DIRECTLY** AFTER **MR. MAGIC** ON **WHBI**.

YOU LOOK LIKE SOME KINDA **PLAYA**...

WE **DOWN**.

PRETTY SOON, FAB GETS YET **ANOTHER** OFFER TO MAKE A RECORD WHEN APPROACHED BY TWO ROXY PATRONS, **JEAN KARAKOS** AND **BERNARD ZEKRI**, FROM THE **AVANT-GARDE** FRENCH MUSIC LABEL **CELLULOID RECORDS**.

... WE WANT TO MAKE A FRENCH RAP RECORD..?

SOUNDS BETTER THAN HOME COOKIN'...

ZEKRI'S BILINGUAL GIRLFRIEND, **ANN BOYLE**, TEACHES FRED THE LYRICS AND THEY ACTUALLY **BOTH** END UP DOING RECORDINGS FOR **CHANGE THE BEAT** WITH FRED ON THE "A" SIDE AND ANN (FAB FIVE **BETTY**) ON THE "BESIDE."

THE VERY END OF THIS "BESIDE" CONTAINS A PHRASE THAT CONTAINS ONE WORD THAT MAKES **CHANGE THE BEAT**, POSSIBLY, THE MOST SAMPLED RECORD IN HISTORY. ALL IT TOOK WAS FAB FIVE FREDDY TO AD-LIB "..THIS STUFF IS REEAALY **FRESHHHH**.." INTO A VOCODER.

FRESH!

F-F-FRESH FRESH!

GRAND MIXER DST!

MEMBER OF THE ZULU NATION

THE UPTOWN/DOWNTOWN CONVERGENCE IS SOMETHING CHARLIE AHEARN WANTS TO CAPTURE WITH HIS FILM, **WILD STYLE**. NOW THAT HE HAS FUNDING FROM, OF ALL PLACES, TV STATIONS IN EUROPE, HE CAN BEGIN SHOOTING THE PICTURE.

...I DON'T THINK I'M GONNA BE IN THE MOVIE. IT SOUNDS KINDA GOOFY.

CHARLIE WANTS GRAFFITI LEGEND **LEE QUINONES** TO BE THE LEAD ACTOR FOR THE PIECE, SO HE PULLS OUT ALL THE STOPS TO GET HIM.

LEE, YOUR GIRLFRIEND IS DEFINITELY DOING THE FILM. DO YOU KNOW THAT THERE'S A KISSING SCENE WITH HER CHARACTER AND YOURS? DO YOU WANT HER KISSING SOME STRANGER?

THE **FIRST** DAY ON SET...

LEE, YOUR FACE IS GONNA BE ON GIGANTIC THEATER SCREENS. COVERING THAT SCAR ON YOUR NOSE WITH MAKEUP WON'T MAKE A DIFFERENCE.

PLAYING LEE'S ON-AGAIN-OFF-AGAIN GIRLFRIEND IN THE FILM IS HIS **REAL LIFE** ON-AGAIN-OFF-AGAIN GIRLFRIEND, **LADY PINK**, A GRAFFITI LEGEND IN HER OWN RIGHT.

SHE'S ON THE JOCK!

A FELLOW GRAFF STAR, **ZEPHYR**, PLAYS **Z-ROC**, AN ARTIST WHO IS SUSPICIOUS OF THE DOWNTOWN SCENE. WORKING DOUBLE-DUTY, ZEPHY IS ALSO RESPONSIBLE FOR THE COOL ANIMATION AT THE BEGINNING OF **WILD STYLE**.

ZORO?!

FAB FIVE FREDDY IS **PHADE**, A CHARACTER WHO PARALLELS THE ACTUAL FRED BY PUSHING FOR THE UPTOWN/DOWNTOWN UNION.

...YOU MIGHT NOT GET THE MONEY, LIKE, **RIGHT NOW**, BUT YOU GONNA HAVE MONEY LIKE **BARRY WHITE**, MAN!

SINCE THERE'S NO BUDGET TO LICENSE EXISTING MUSIC, IT'S UP TO FRED TO HELP ORCHESTRATE INSTRUMENTALS FOR THE FILM. HE ENLISTS THE HELP OF **CHRIS STEIN**, FROM BLONDIE, TO HELP CREATE SOME FRESH BREAK BEATS.

SOUNDS GREAT! I HAVE SOME PALS WHO'LL HELP, TOO!

FABRICATING A DOZEN OR SO TRACKS TO PLAY AROUND WITH, THEY PRESS UP ENOUGH VINYL TO GIVE **GRANDMASTER FLASH, GRANDWIZARD THEODORE, GRANDMIXER DST., KOOL DJ AJ, TONY TONE, AND CHARLIE CHASE** TWO COPIES APIECE.

PARTICIPATING **MC'S** AND **DJ'S** ARE INSTRUCTED TO CHOOSE A TRACK FOR THEIR OWN USE AND TO FORMULATE A PERFORMANCE FOR THE FILM.

WHERE'S THE PLACE WE WORK IT OUT?

AT THE **ALPS!**

AT THE **ALPS!**

AT THE **ALPS!**

AT THE **ALPS!**

THE **ALPS HOTEL**, FROM THE NOTORIOUS **BUSY BEE STARSKI** ROUTINE, IS ACTUALLY USED AS A LOCATION IN THE FILMING OF **WILDSTYLE**.

I WANTED TO GO TO THE **HYATT**, AND THEY SAID THEY WAS GON' TAKE US THERE...

...I THOUGHT THEY HAD SOME MONEY, BUT I SEE THEY STARVIN'!

25% OF THE BUDGET (AROUND $20,000) IS USED TO SECURE PERMISSION TO ACCESS THE **MTA YARD** FOR A FEW SCENES.

!?

THERE AIN'T NO WAY YOU'RE GONNA FILM ME PAINTIN' HERE, MAN!

GRAFFITI PIONEER **DONDI WHITE** ENDS UP STANDING IN FOR LEE AND EXECUTES THE PAINTING ON THE TRAIN.

THE EUROPEAN TV STATIONS, **ZDF** IN **WEST GERMANY** AND **CHANNEL 4** IN THE **UK**, WHOSE INVESTMENTS MAKE THE BULK OF THE BUDGET, SEND AN **EXECUTIVE** TO SEE HOW THINGS ARE GOING.

STOP!

POLICE!

REIMAGINING THE EARLIER **EPIC** BATTLE AT **HARLEM WORLD** BETWEEN THE **COLD CRUSH BROTHERS** AND THE **FANTASTIC FIVE**, CHARLIE AHEARN CONSTRUCTS A MOMENT FOR HIS FILM THAT'S STRAIGHT OUT OF WEST SIDE STORY.

CHARLIE, I NEED TO DO THAT ONE AGAIN. I WASN'T FEELIN' IT.

C'MON, MAN...

UGH, NOT AGAIN!!

IT TAKES THEM 18 TAKES FOR EVERYONE TO HIT THEIR MARKS.

TO DO EACH GROUP JUSTICE, **WILD STYLE** ALSO FEATURES THEM PERFORMING IN THE DARKROOM-LIKE ATMOSPHERE OF A CLUB CALLED **THE DIXIE**.

...AND WE'RE PLEASIN' ALL THE LADIEEEEEEEEEZ...

ASHES TO ASHES AND DUST TO DUST, WE ARE THE FOUR KNOWN AS THE COL' CRUSH...

FEATURED PROMINENTLY AT THIS POINT IN THE FLICK IS **PATTI ASTOR** AS A NEWS REPORTER. IN REAL LIFE SHE'S A FIXTURE ON THE DOWNTOWN SCENE, AND AN ACTRESS IN MANY UNDERGROUND NEW YORK FILMS.

IN CIVILIAN LIFE, SHE ALSO RUNS THE **FUN GALLERY**, WHICH PROMOTES RISING ART STARS LIKE **KEITH HARING** AND **JEAN-MICHEL BASQUIAT**.

...OOOH, WHAT'S YOUR NEW GIRL- FRIEND'S NAME?

MADONNA.

23

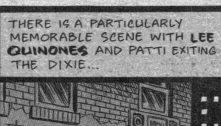

THERE IS A PARTICULARLY MEMORABLE SCENE WITH **LEE QUINONES** AND PATTI EXITING THE DIXIE...

CHARLIE AHEARN WANTS TO SHOW PEOPLE THAT DESPITE THE PARTY VIBE OF **HIP HOP**, THERE STILL IS AN ELEMENT OF DANGER IN THE **BRONX**.

HEY, WOULD YOU GUYS LIKE TO BE IN THE MOVIE?

HERE. TAKE THIS. I WANT YOU TO MENACE THESE TWO, LIKE THEY DON'T BELONG IN YOUR NEIGHBORHOOD.

?

THE MAN ASSURES CHARLIE THAT HE HAS A WAY BETTER WEAPON FOR THE FILM IN HIS CAR.

I CAN'T USE THIS...

...THIS IS A **PUSSY** GUN.

...YOU'VE HEARD IT ON THE **RADIO**, YOU'VE SEEN IT ON A TV **SHOW**...

"A" TO THE "**K**"?

"A" TO THE MUTHAFUCKIN' "C"!!

SAWED-OFF!

AHEARN FEELS IT'S IMPOLITE TO ASK IF THE GUN IS **EMPTY** WHILE THE GENTLEMEN ARE AD-LIBBING THEIR PERFORMANCES.

BELIEVING DEEPLY IN **WILDSTYLE**, **BLONDIE** IS MORE THAN HAPPY TO ALLOW **FAB FIVE FREDDY** AND **CHARLIE AHEARN** TO USE THEIR SONG, **RAPTURE**, FOR THE SOCIALITE, ART-GATHERING SCENE THAT IS USED TO INTEGRATE **LEE QUINONES** WITH THE **DOWNTOWN** CROWD.

CAN I CALL YOU **ZORO**?

NO, NO. IT WOULD BE BETTER OFF IF YOU JUS' CALL ME **RAYMOND**.

GLENN O'BRIEN, THE HOST OF THE PUBLIC ACCESS SHOW **TV PARTY**, EDITOR OF WARHOL'S **INTER-VIEW MAGAZINE**, AND CATALYST FOR INTRODUCING FRED TO THE **VILLAGE VOICE**, PLAYS THE STUFFED-SHIRT MANAGER OF THE **WHITNEY MUSEUM**.

WE'VE SPENT $50,000 REMOVING GRAFFITI FROM THE FACADE OF OUR BUILDING...

THIS PART OF THE FLICK TAKES PLACE AT **NIVA KISLAC'S** APARTMENT. SHE TRULY IS A BIG-TIME ART COLLECTOR WHO SEES VALUE IN GRAFFITI, BUYING **BASQUIATS** AND **FAB FIVES** TO HANG NEXT TO HER **FRANK STELLAS**.

THE END OF THIS SCENE BASHFULLY CALLS FOR LEE TO BE **SEDUCED** BY NIVA.

DON'T BE FRIGHTENED. IT'S OKAY. SIT DOWN. PLEASE.

THE SCENE **DOESN'T** CALL FOR LEE'S GIRLFRIEND, **LADY PINK**, TO BE THERE, BUT SHE SHOWS UP ANYWAY.

KEEPING THEIR PROMISE TO **K.K. ROCKWELL** AND **LITTLE RODNEY C** AFTER THE DEMISE OF THE **FUNKY FOUR PLUS ONE**, FAB AND CHARLIE INCLUDE THE DUO IN YET ANOTHER ICONIC SCENE IN WILD STYLE. THE FREESTYLE THEY PERFORM ON THE STOOP IS INDICATIVE OF THEIR STRIFE WITH THE **SUGAR HILL** RECORD LABEL.

HERE'S A LITTLE STORY THAT MUST BE **TOLD**...

...ABOUT TWO COOL BROTHERS WHO WERE PUT ON **HOLD**...

...TRIED TO HOLD US BACK FROM FORTUNE AND **FAME**, THEY DE-STROYED THE CREW AND THEY KILLED THE **NAME**...

...THEY TRIED TO STEP ON THE EGO AND WALK ON THE **PRIDE**...

K.K. ROCKWELL

...BUT **TRUE-BLUE** BROTHERS STAND **SIDE** BY **SIDE**...

RODNEY C.

"...THROUGH... THICK AND **THIN**. FROM BEGINNING TO EN'..."

"...THE BATTLE WE LOST BUT THE WAR WE'LL **WIN**..."

RODNEY C'S HOUSE IS VERY NEAR THE SET AND THE CREW TAKES FULL ADVANTAGE OF THE SITUATION.

THANKS SO MUCH, MS. STONE!

THE RAP BEING BELTED OUT ON THE VIGNETTE BEFORE THE FINAL SCENES IS PERFORMED BY **GRANDMASTER CAZ** OVER ONE OF THOSE CONSTRUCTED **CHRIS STEIN** RIFFS.

"LOOK PAST THE GARBAGE, OVER THE **TRAINS**, UNDER THE RUINS, THROUGH THE **REMAINS**..."

"...AROUND THE CRIME AND **POLLUTION** AND TELL ME, WHERE DO I FIT **IN**..."

"...SOUTH BRONX, NEW YORK, THAT'S WHERE I **DWELL** TO A LOT OF PEOPLE IT'S A LIVING **HELL**..."

WILD STYLE'S CLIMAX IS MEANT TO BE A BIG SHOW AT THIS **AMPHITHEATER** ON **AVENUE D**. BUT, DESPITE CHARLIE AHEARN'S CONSTANT PRODDING, THE CITY PARKS COMMISSION KEEPS GIVING HIM THE RUN-AROUND.

AFTER A YEAR OF TRYING AND FUSSING, THE FILM CREW DECIDES TO MOVE FORWARD ILLEGALLY.

THEY ACTUALLY HAVE TO FILM THE AMPHITHEATER SCENE ON **TWO** OCCASIONS BECAUSE OF **POOR** SOUND QUALITY. **GRANDMASTER FLASH AND THE FURIOUS FIVE** PLAYED THE FIRST ROUND, BUT DIDN'T FEEL LIKE PLAYING THE DAY THAT ENDED UP IN THE MOVIE. **FLASH'S** MEMORABLE SCENE WAS MEANT TO LEAD UP TO THE GROUP'S PERFORMANCE. IT SHOULD BE NOTED THAT THIS **IS** FLASH'S **KITCHEN** AND THAT HE OPTS **NOT** TO USE A PREFABRICATED BEAT BY CHRIS STEIN, CHOOSING INSTEAD A HIP HOP STAPLE, **TAKE ME TO THE MARDI GRAS** BY BOB JAMES.

DURING FLASH'S **3-TURNTABLE** TOUR DE-FORCE, AHEARN EDITS A MONTAGE DEMONSTRATING OTHER ELEMENTS OF HIP HOP CULTURE, LIKE THE **B BOY** VIRTUOSITY OF THE **ROCK STEADY CREW**...

CRAZY LEGS!

... AND **LEE QUINONES** IN ACTION WITH RATTLE-CANS AT THE AMPHITHEATER.

DAYS BEFORE THE BIG EVENT, **FAB FIVE FREDDY** MAKES THE ROUNDS TO PROMOTE THE SHOW BY VISITING NEIGHBORING PROJECTS.

COLD CRUSH. FANTASTIC... EVERY-ONE'S GONNA BE THERE.

STYLE!

WILD STYLE

A HIP HOP FAN FROM **CON EDISON** ILLEGALLY RIGS THE ELECTRICITY TO THE GENERATORS, AMPS, AND SPEAKERS REQUIRED FOR THE BIG PRODUCTION.

... AND YA DON'T STOP!

THOUSANDS OF PEOPLE SHOW UP TO SEE THE AMAZING PERFORMERS ON THE BILL.

THIS, OF COURSE, SPARKS THE INTEREST OF **LAW ENFORCEMENT**.

HEY, THANKS FOR COMING DOWN, OFFICER. DO YOU MIND RUNNING **SECURITY**? WE HAVE A BIGGER AUDIENCE THAN WE EXPECTED...

249

NOT ANOTHER COP COMES WITHIN MILES OF THE SHOOT FOR THE REST OF THE NIGHT.

FANTASTIC ROMANTIC FREAKS IN THE HOUSE!

THE **AMPHITHEATER** IN THE FINAL SCENE IS NEAR **AVENUE D**, ALPHABET CITY IN THE L.E.S. OF **MANHATTAN**.

AVENUE A, YOU ALL RIGHT.

AVENUE B, BE CARE-FUL!

AVENUE C, YOU CRAZY!

AVENUE D, YOU DEAD!!

THE **FANTASTIC FIVE** SETS THE TEMPO AS THEY RUSH THE STAGE THROUGH THE CROWD.

HELLOOO, EVERYBODY!!!

THEN COMES **BUSY BEE STARSKI**, WHO GETS THE CROWD ON HIS SIDE WITH A REFERENCE TO **WAYNE WILLIAMS**, THE SERIAL KILLER WHO'S ALL OVER THE NEWS AT THE TIME OF THE FILMING.

...AN' SMACK THE **HELL** OUT OF IT LIKE **THIS!**

EVEN THE PEOPLE ON STAGE ARE UNDER **BUSY BEE'S** SPELL, LISTENING TO HIS EVERY **COMMAND**... EXCEPT FOR **KOOL MOE DEE** IN HIS STOIC B-BOY STANCE.

...C'MON CLAP... **CLAP** YOUR HANDS!

DOUBLE TROUBLE, RODNEY C AND K.K. ROCKWELL, REPRISE THEIR **STOOP RAP** WITH GREAT STYLE.

AN UNMASKED **RAMMELLZEE** IS THE EMCEE WITH THE UNORTHODOX **FLOW** PROMOTING THE **ROCK STEADY CREW.**

IT'S A GREAT OPPORTUNITY FOR **FROSTY FREEZE** TO SHOWCASE HIS POWER MOVE, THE **SUICIDE!**

NILE ROGERS FROM THE BAND **CHIC** SIGNS OFF ON **GRANDMIXER DST**'S USE OF **GOOD TIMES** WHEN KOOL MOE DEE GETS ON THE MIC.

ONE FOR THE **TREBLE**, TWO FOR THE **TIME**... C'MON Y'ALL LET'S HAVE A... GOOD TIMES!

IF YOU HAVE A KEEN EYE YOU'LL NOTICE **MOE DEE** IS JOINED BY **MR. MAGIC** HELPING TO GET THE CROWD INTO A **FRENZY.**

JUMP! JUMP!!

LA SUNSHINE OF THE **TREACHEROUS THREE** CLOSES OUT THE FILM.

WE WANT EVERYBODY TO COME CHECK THE MOVIE, HOWEVER IT TURN OUT!

BEHIND THE SCENES, DIRECTOR **CHARLIE AHEARN** IS PASSING OUT ONE-HUNDRED-DOLLAR BILLS TO PERFORMERS COMING OFF STAGE.

IF WE **DIDN'T** CAPTURE THE SOUND PROPERLY THIS TIME WE'RE **FUCKED!**

THIS BURNT-OUT ABANDONED BUILDING AT **171 AVENUE A** BECOMES THE EPICENTER OF THE NEW YORK CITY **HARDCORE-PUNK** MOVEMENT.

WHEN **JERRY WILLIAMS** COMES ACROSS THE DILAPIDATED STRUCTURE, A FORMER GLASS SHOP, HE TAKES SEVERAL MONTHS TO CLEAR THE MAIN ROOM AND ERECT A STAGE, WHICH QUICKLY GAINS THE ATTENTION OF EVERYBODY IN THE SCENE.

AFTER THE FIRE DEPT. SHUTS DOWN THE SHOWS AT 171A, WHICH WERE ILLEGAL WITHOUT A LIQUOR LICENSE, THE SPACE MORPHS INTO A PRACTICE/RECORDING STUDIO. THE **BAD BRAINS** LIVE AND RECORD THEIR FIRST ALBUM HERE.

THIS VENUE IS ALSO WHERE **BLACK FLAG** SPENDS TIME AUDITIONING **HENRY ROLLINS** TO BECOME THEIR NEW SINGER.

THE **BASEMENT** OF THE BUILDING IS USED BY **DAVE PARSONS** TO RUN HIS STORE, **RAT CAGE RECORDS**.

YEAH? WHATCHA LOOKIN' FOR?

UH, GOT ANY WEED IN HERE, MAN?

31

AT THIS STAGE, **JOHN BERRY** MIGHT BE THE MOST IMPORTANT MEMBER OF THE **HARDCORE** BAND THE **BEASTIE BOYS**. IF IT WASN'T FOR THE PARTY AT BERRY'S HOUSE, **PARSONS** MIGHT NOT HAVE SEEN THE BEASTIES PERFORM.

EGG RAID ON MOJO!

PARSONS HAD BEEN WANTING TO CREATE A **LABEL** FOR SOME TIME, AND ON A DAY WHEN **THE CIRCLE JERKS, ANGRY SAMOANS,** OR **THE SUBHUMANS** AREN'T USING THE FACILITIES, DAVE IS ABLE TO RECORD THE **BEASTIE BOYS** AT **171A**.

RI-RI-RIOT FIGHT!!

CUT! MICHAEL, QUIT TOUCHIN' THE MIC, MAN!!

THROUGH THE NEW **RAT CAGE RECORDS** LABEL, THE BEASTIE BOYS (**ADAM YAUCH, MICHAEL DIAMOND, KATE SCHELLENBACH,** AND **JOHN BERRY**) RELEASE THEIR **FIRST** RECORD, AN 8-SONG, HARDCORE-PUNK E.P.

POLLY WOG STEW · E.P.

THIS INSPIRES PARSONS TO RECORD ANOTHER SHORT ALBUM OF THE SAME ILK. HE PRESSES **800 COPIES** OF **REAL MEN DON'T FLOSS** BY **THE YOUNG AND THE USELESS**, A BAND OF BRATTY TEENS THAT INCLUDES **ADAM HOROVITZ** ON GUITAR.

ADAM HOROVITZ

THE OTHER VERY IMPORTANT CIRCUMSTANCE CREATED BY BEASTIE BOY **JOHN BERRY** IS WHEN HE GOES **AWOL** FROM THE BAND, OPENING THE SLOT FOR A GUITAR PLAYER, WHICH IS RAPIDLY FILLED BY **ADAM HOROVITZ**, WHO PING PONGS BETWEEN **BOTH** BANDS FOR A WHILE.

HA HA...

HOLY PISS, HOLY CRAPPERS!

JILL CUNIFF! HOLY SNAPPERS!

GRANDMASTER FLASHBACK 1979...

HOW MUCH DO YOU WANT FOR IT?

$125

AT PRACTICE WITH THE FURIOUS 5...

THIS **DRUMMER** GUY I KNOW USED THIS TO **PRACTICE** WHENEVER HE DIDN'T FEEL LIKE BANGIN' ON HIS KIT.

SEE, THERE ARE **BUTTONS** FOR THE BASS DRUM, THE **HI-HAT**... HERE'S THE **SNARE**!!

WHAT IS IT?

IT'S A DRUM MACHINE BUT I CALL IT A **BEAT BOX.**

EVERY SPARE MOMENT...

BOOP BOOP OOMP BOPP BOOP BOOP

AFTER A FEW MONTHS THE FURIOUS CREATE ROUTINES AROUND THIS ADDITIONAL INSTRUMENT...

LISTEN TO THIS... LISTEN TO THIS... LISTEN... LISTEN... LISTEN TO THIS...

BOOP BOP

WITH THIS NEW WEAPON **GRANDMASTER FLASH AND THE FURIOUS FIVE** ARE INVITED BY **AFRIKA BAMBAATAA** TO PLAY A **ZULU NATION** JAM AT THE BRONX RIVER COMMUNITY CENTER.

...AND IT WON'T BE LONG 'TIL EVERYBODY KNOW THAT FLASH WAS ON THE BEATBOX GOIN'... BOOP BOOP

BAMBAATAA HAS **NEVER** SEEN SUCH A **FUNKY** GIZMO, BUT HE IS **FAMILIAR** WITH THE SOUND FROM BANDS LIKE **KRAFTWERK** AND OTHER MORE **EXPERIMENTAL** RECORDS.

GLAD I'M RECORDING THIS...

MAYBE THROUGH **COMMERCE**, MAYBE FROM **TRADING**, MAYBE BECAUSE OF **THEFT** THE TAPE **LEAKS** AND THIS PERFORMANCE CIRCULATES LIKE WILDFIRE FOR **YEARS** IN THE HIP HOP COMMUNITY.

YO, **RUN**, WE NEED TO GET US A **ROCK BOX.**

DARRYL McDANIELS

BEAT BOX!

BOOP

WHAT THE HELL IS THIS?

GRANDMASTER FLASH FORWARD TO 1982: THE **LEGENDARY** TAPE IS RE-LEASED ON VINYL THROUGH THE MYSTERIOUS **BOZO MEKO** RECORD LABEL AND **SUGAR HILL** OWNER **SYLVIA ROBINSON** IS NOT HAPPY ABOUT THIS AT **ALL**.

THE **BOOTLEG** IS A MULTI-GENERATION DUPLICATE. IT'S GRITTY. YOU CAN HEAR ALL SORTS OF RESIDUAL NOISE. IT'S FAR FROM **PERFECT**, BUT IT MIGHT BE ONE OF THE GREATEST SNAPSHOTS OF HIP HOP **BEFORE** THE MUSIC BECOMES BIG BUSINESS.

...BUT AN INDUSTRY HAS SPRUNG UP IN THE YEARS AFTER THAT INITIAL TAPE RECORDING, SO SYLVIA SEES THIS AS AN **OPPORTUNITY**. SHE RUSHES FLASH AND THE FURIOUS FIVE INTO THE **STUDIO** TO REINTERPRET THE **FLASH TO THE BEAT** ROUTINES. THEY USE THE **FINEST** RECORDING EQUIPMENT, INSTRUMENTATION, MICROPHONES, AND OTHER TECHNOLOGY TO CREATE A **PRISTINE** EXPERIENCE, AND IN DOING SO, THEY SOMEHOW BOIL OUT THE **HEART AND SOUL** OF THE 1979 PERFORMANCE FROM THE **BRONX RIVER PROJECTS**.

AS A **FLY** ASIDE, THE **B-SIDE** TO THE BOZO MEKO **FLASH IT TO THE BEAT** IS AN EXTREMELY DANCEABLE MEDLEY CALLED **FUSION BEATS VOL. 2**. BAMBAATAA, **JAZZY JAY**, AND **AFRIKA ISLAM** (AKA THE SON OF BAMBAATAA) SEAMLESSLY WEAVE TOGETHER CORE HIP HOP RECORDS LIKE **THE CHAMP** BY THE MOHAWKS, **GET UP, GET INTO IT, GET INVOLVED** BY **JAMES BROWN**, AND MORE...

DYKE AND THE BLAZERS!

THE **COLD CRUSH BROTHERS** HAVE RELENTLESSLY BEEN PLAYING PARKS, GYMS, PARTIES, AND CLUBS FOR YEARS. TAKING ON ALL COMERS, THEIR **MANTLE** IN THE STREETS IS SEALED. THEY HAVEN'T PURSUED A RECORD DEAL YET. CIVIC POPULARITY IS THEIR MAIN FOCUS.

I WRITE THE RHYMES THAT ARE **BEST**...

...AN' I FLAKE OUT AT EMCEE **CONTESTS**...

...I SNATCH ALL THE GIRLS...

...I SNIFF ALL THE BLOW...

GRANDMASTER CAZ

ALMIGHTY KG

JDL

EASY A.D.

ARTHUR ARMSTRONG, THE OWNER OF A POPULAR CLUB THEY PLAY, WANTS TO DO SOMETHING ABOUT THE **CC4**'S VOID ON WAX.

SURE, WHY NOT.

BEFORE BOOKING THE STUDIO TIME...

WE OUGHTTA **RECORD** THE ROUTINE WHERE WE BURNT THE **FORCE MC'S**.

NAW, THE ONE WHERE WE MADE **FANTASTIC** LOOK STUPID!

CHARLIE CHASE

ONY ONE

ARTHUR DECIDES THEY SHOULD CREATE A SONG AROUND A THEME. THIS IS WHERE **GRANDMASTER CAZ**, THE LEAD MC OF THE COLD CRUSH, COMES IN.

I GOT RHYMES BY THE DOZENS!

FOLLOWING THE MODEL OF THE DAY, ARMSTRONG BRINGS IN A LIVE BAND FOR THE MUSIC.

DJ CHARLIE CHASE

THIS HAPPENED BEFORE! *

DJ TONY TONE

* WITH THE **FUNKY FOUR**, HHFT#1

DUE TO THE EXPENSE OF USING A **PROFESSIONAL** STUDIO, TIME IS BEYOND LIMITED.

IT'S GOOD ENOUGH.

THE RESULTING FEW HOURS YIELD **WEEKEND** BY THE COLD CRUSH BROTHERS. AN EVERYMAN SONG ABOUT WORKING HARD AND PARTYING ON YOUR FREE TIME.

YO, **D**, IS THIS THE SAME **COL' CRUSH**?

THINK SO...

THIS **COMPROMISED** VISION DOESN'T REACH FAR BEYOND THE **FIVE BOROUGHS**, BUT IT DOES SELL A FEW THOUSAND COPIES IN THE REGION. ANOTHER CONCEIT OF THE DAY IS THAT VINYL TRANSCENDS THE PERFORMER BEYOND THE **GHETTO** INTO A ROCKSTAR, AND IT'S AN OPINION THE **COLD CRUSH** ARE COMFORTABLE ADOPTING.

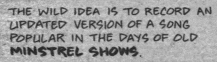

MALCOLM McLAREN THINKS THERE IS NO TIME LIKE THE PRESENT TO INTRODUCE **HIP HOP** MUSIC TO HIS MOTHERLAND OF **ENGLAND**.

WORLD'S FAMOUS SUPREME TEAM, WELCOME!

YOUR MONEY BE GOOD.

THE **WILD** IDEA IS TO RECORD AN UPDATED VERSION OF A SONG POPULAR IN THE DAYS OF OLD **MINSTREL SHOWS**.

GOOD DAY, GENTLEMEN. HERE ARE YOUR "**RAPS**."

SAY WHA?

BOOKING A STUDIO IN ENGLAND, McLAREN SOLICITS THE SERVICE OF **TREVOR HORN**, THE BEST **PRODUCER** HE CAN THINK OF.

AIN'T NO WAY!!

WE CAN'T DO NO KU KLUX KLAN RHYMES! SHIT'S WACK!!

FORGIVE ME, KIND SIR, BUT IS "**WACK**" A GOOD OR BAD THING?

..TRIPPIN'.

IT'S BAD!!

VERY GOOD.

..UM, DOES "BAD" MEAN "GOOD"?

TREVOR BRINGS WITH HIM STATE-OF-THE-ART **DRUM MACHINES** TO WHIP THE **BEAT** INTO SHAPE.

IT GOTTA SOUND LIKE: ≺BA BOD OMP≻ ≺BA BOMP≻.

BA BA BOD OMP

NO NO NO!

McLAREN'S **VOCALS** ADD EVEN MORE COMPLEXITY TO THE MIX.

HA HA!!

MALCOLM! HA HAW YOU'ZA **VIBE** KILLA!

ONCE BACK IN NYC, THE **WORLD'S FAMOUS SUPREME TEAM** DECIDES THEY AREN'T HAPPY WITH THEIR **SCRATCH** PERFORMANCE.

WE CAN'T.

DON'T **WORRY**, CHAP. IT'S MORE A **PUNK** RECORD, REALLY.

OH, OKAY, HEY, WOULD YOU GIVE US THAT DRUM MACHINE AS A **BONUS**?

NO SIR. IT COST £2000. SORRY.

THE **CULTURAL COLLISION** BEARS THE RECORD **BUFFALO GALS**, CREATING THE EXACT EFFECT MALCOLM McLAREN HAD IN MIND.

..AND DOSEY DOE YUH PARTNER!

?

IT'S GREAT, RIGHT?

36

JUNEBUG IS THE HOUSE DJ FOR THE BRONX'S MOST **SOPHISTICATED** HIP HOP NIGHTCLUB, THE **DISCO FEVER**. WITH ACCESS TO SUCH AN AUDIENCE, MIXING RECORDS SOON BECAME A **SIDE BUSINESS** FOR JUNEBUG.

SAL, CAN YOU HOLD THIS FOR ME?

HOLY SHIT!! WHERE'D YOU GET ALL THIS? HOW MUCH IS HERE, ANYWAY?

$3500. I MADE IT WHILE WORKIN' THE BOOTH.

MAN, WE **ONLY** TOOK IN ABOUT **$1500** TODAY...

...I'M **NOT** STUPID, JUNEBUG! I **KNOW** YOU'RE SELLIN' **SHIT** BUT THIS IS TOO MUCH. I **THOUGHT** YOU WERE JUST INTO 10'S AND 15'S. NOT THIS MUCH!

SAL ABBATIELLO AND THE DISCO FEVER HAVE BEEN LONGTIME **SPONSORS** OF MR. MAGIC'S FAMED RADIO SHOW, **DISCO SHOWCASE**, AND IN THAT TIME THEY'VE BUILT A **GENUINE** FRIENDSHIP.

JUNEBUG'S GOT ME WORRIED. HE'S A FUCKING **DJ**, NOT A **DRUG DEALER**.

DON'T SWEAT IT.

ON TOP OF ALL HIS **OTHER** ACTIVITIES, JUNEBUG IS **ALSO** MR. MAGIC'S **DJ** ON THE RADIO, SPINNING VINYL AT MAGIC'S **COMMAND**.

SPEAKIN' OF WHICH, I NEED TO HEAD OVER TO 'BUG'S PAD TO PICK UP A LIL SOME-SOME.

SAL GETS **HASSLED** REGULARLY BY THE **COPS**, AND IT FORCES HIM TO LEAD A VERY **CAREFUL** LIFE. HE NEVER THOUGHT THAT HIS **TALENTED** AND **JOVIAL** HOUSE DJ WOULD ADD **COMPLICATION** TO HIS SITUATION.

HEY, **MAGIC**. JUNEBUG BE IN THE BACK ROOM.

THANKS, LAMAR.

AS THE **LEGEND** GOES, WE FIND A YOUNG **LAWRENCE** AND **KENNY** PARKER...

BUT, I DON'T **WANT** RICE-A-RONI, **LARRY**.

'SALL WE GOT.

MOM GETS HOME AFTER A HARD DAY'S WORK...

THAT WAS **OUR** DINNER! **GIT OUT!** I DON'T EVEN WANNA **LOOKIT** YO' FACES RIGHT NOW!!

THEY USUALLY HAVE BEANS, RICE, AND BREAD ON THEIR SHELF.

HOURS GO BY...

KENNY, MAN. YOU WAS **HUNGRIER** THAN I WAS.

NO, YOU WAS!

MORE TIME PASSES...

WHAT WOULD **YOU** DO WITH **$1000**? I THINK I'D BUY MY OWN CRIB.

HMMM, I **THINK** I'D MAKE A RAP REKKID LIKE **FLASH** AN' 'EM.

AND SO ON...

DAYS LATER...

MOM **SHOULD** BE FINE NOW, YA THINK?

YEAH, **KENNY**. GO **HOME** AN' GET **FRESH**.

WHEN SHOULD I TELL MOM YOU'RE COMIN' BACK?

I'M **NOT** GONNA, KEN. **PEACE**, BRUH.

ON A **DAILY** BASIS, DURING BUSINESS HOURS...

TOMMY BOY RECORDS HAS BEEN INTERESTED IN PUTTING TOGETHER A **NEW** SINGLE WITH **AFRIKA BAMBAATAA** FOR A WHILE.

THERE AIN'T NO **BLACK** ELECTRONIC GROUPS OUT THERE LIKE **KRAFTWERK**.

I WANNA MAKE SOMETHING FOR THE **PUNK ROCKERS** AND THE **HIP HOP** KIDS.

PRODUCER **ARTHUR BAKER** AGREES THAT SUCH A RECORD CAN'T BE MADE **WITHOUT** THE USE OF A **DRUM MACHINE**. BAM AND BAKER BOTH LIKE THE SOUND OF THE **TR-808**, BUT THEY DON'T KNOW ANYBODY WHO HAS ONE.

HA! WHO'D HAVE THUNK IT?

"JOE" REQUIRES $20 AN HOUR BEFORE HE'LL PROGRAM HIS TR-808 FOR A NEW PROJECT.

CASH PLEASE!

I **DON'T** ACCEPT CHECKS FROM LABELS I'VE **NEVER** HEARD OF.

THEY **EXPERIMENT** WITH A HANDFUL OF BEATS LIKE **SUPER SPERM** BY **CAPTAIN SKY**. THE **DOMINANT** SOUNDS COME WHEN THEY ELECTRONICALLY CONSTRUCT RIFFS FROM **KRAFTWERK** LIKE **TRANS-EUROPE EXPRESS** AND **NUMBERS**.

THEY SPEND THE **WHOLE** FIRST DAY CREATING THE **INSTRUMENTAL**, WHICH TURNS OUT TO BE THE EASY PART OF THE OPERATION.

HONEY...

...WE MADE **FUCKIN'** MUSICAL HISTORY TODAY!

THE RAPPERS FROM BAMBAATAA'S **SOUL SONIC FORCE** AREN'T AS ENTHUSIASTIC ABOUT THE PROSPECTS BECAUSE IT'S SO **DIFFERENT** FROM WHAT THEY'RE USED TO. EMCEE **POW-WOW** DOESN'T EVEN REMEMBER ALL HIS LINES.

ZIH-ZIH-ZIH-ZIH-ZAH
ZIH-ZIH-ZAH! ZI-ZI-ZI
ZIH-ZIH-ZIH-ZAH!

PLANET ROCK EMERGES FROM THE STUDIO SESSION WITH AFRIKA BAMBAATAA AND THE SOUL SONIC FORCE AT A RECORDING COST OF $800. ADOPTED BY UPTOWN AND DOWNTOWN SCENES, THE RECORD SELLS 650,000 COPIES AND GETS CERTIFIED GOLD ON SEPTEMBER 16, 1982.

AFRIKA BAMBAATAA

MR. BIGGS

G.L.O.B.E.

POW WOW

THE POPULARITY OF THE SONG DOESN'T ESCAPE THE EARS OF THE KRAFTWERK BANDMATES.

THEY WANT A 25¢ ROYALTY ON EVERY RECORD SOLD!

I DON'T THINK SO!

TOM SILVERMAN

CEO OF TOMMY BOY RECORDS

TOMMY BOY AGREES TO PAY KRAFTWERK 17¢ PER RECORD SOLD AND CONCOCTS A SCHEME TO MAKE UP FOR THE LOSS.

WHY DOES PLANET ROCK COST A DOLLAR MORE THAN EVERY-THING ELSE?

'CUZ IT'S AWE-SOME!

"JOE," THE GUY WITH THE SKILLS ON THE TR-808, COULDN'T BE FOUND AND HASN'T EVEN TRIED TO COLLECT ROYALTIES, HIMSELF. DOES HE KNOW WHAT HE WAS A PART OF

THE **MIDDLE** PART OF A FEW DAYS WORTH OF **PARTYING**...

SHIT! I JUST REALIZED I BEST CHECK IN WITH MY **MOMS**, LET 'ER KNOW I'M STILL **ALIVE**.

SAY WHA?

REALLY?

PAYPHONE

INDOOR PUBLIC ASHTRAY

Y'ALL WON'T BELIEVE THIS! **FRANKIE CROCKER** CALLED THE **CRIB**!

'BOUT **TIME** HE JUMPED ON THE **DICK**, MAGIC.

FRANKIE "HOLLYWOOD" CROCKER IS THE MOST SUCCESSFUL BLACK **RADIO** DJ BROADCASTING FROM THE #1 **BLACK** RADIO STATION IN NEW YORK. UP TO THIS POINT HE'S BEEN HARSHLY RESISTANT TO BREAKING **RAP RECORDS** ON **HIS** AIRWAVES.

FRANKIE IS ALSO **PROGRAM DIRECTOR** AT HIS RADIO STATION **WBLS**, WHICH GIVES HIM THE CACHE TO GIVE **MR. MAGIC** THE OPPORTUNITY OF A LIFE-TIME, **UNEXPECTED** AS IT SEEMS. RATHER THAN DOING **DISCO SHOW-CASE** ON PUBLIC RADIO **WHBI** AND **PAYING** FOR THE PRIVILEGE WITH THE HELP OF SPONSORS, MAGIC ACCEPTS **$750** A WEEK TO BROADCAST EVERY FRIDAY AND SATURDAY NIGHT ON **WBLS**. **MR. MAGIC'S RAP ATTACK** AIRS FOR THE FIRST TIME IN **MAY 1982**.

THESE KIDS DON'T HAVE **NO** MONEY TO SPEND...

...AN' THE **ADVERTISERS** ALL KNOW IT!

AIN'T ONE **BROKE** GIZMO IN THIS BITCH!

JALIL, A DR. PEPPER'D BE **GREAT**, BRUTHA.

ON AIR

JIVE RECORDS, A RECENTLY FORMED **BRITISH** LABEL, WANTS TO DO THEIR OWN **RAP** RELEASE. THE NYC AFFILIATES DON'T PER-SONALLY KNOW ANY RAPPERS, **BUT** THEY ARE FAMILIAR WITH MAGIC'S **RADIO SHOW**.

SIGN ME UP!

MR. MAGIC IS **REMINDED** THAT HE CAN'T TAKE THE **RECORD DEAL** FOR FEAR OF IT BEING A **PAYOLA** RACKET.

BEING ON A **BIGGER** RADIO STATION AIN'T ALL IT'S CRACKED UP TO BE! I **HATE** THAT I CAN'T ACCEPT MY OWN **SPONSORS** ANYMORE, EITHER! SOME WEEKS BACK THEN I COULD MAKE **MORE** THAN **$750** A WEEK!

SINCE **JIVE** DOESN'T HAVE A CLUE, MAGIC IS HAPPY TO REACH OUT TO OTHER **ARTISTS** FOR THIS CHANCE, BUT ALL THE **BEST** RAPPERS ARE **BOUND** BY **CONTRACTS**.

WHAT ABOUT **ME**, BOSS?

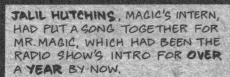

JALIL HUTCHINS, MAGIC'S INTERN, HAD PUT A SONG TOGETHER FOR MR. MAGIC, WHICH HAD BEEN THE RADIO SHOW'S INTRO FOR **OVER A YEAR** BY NOW.

..THINK **YOU** CAN COMPETE WIT' **MELLE MEL** AN' **KOOL MOE DEE** ?

I'LL TAKE ON THE **WORLD** FOR A CHANCE TO GET ON!

WITH MAGIC'S **BLESSING**, JALIL IS ACCEPTED BY **JIVE** TO BE **THEIR** RAPPER. IMAGE-BREAKER **THOMAS DOLBY** IS HIRED TO PRODUCE THE MUSIC FOR THE **RECORD**.

SCIENCE!

ALMOST RIGHT AWAY THERE ARE SPEEDBUMPS ONCE IT COMES TO THE **VOCALS**...

NAW, I DON'T HAVE **NUTHIN'** WRITTEN DOWN.

MY HOMEBOY **ECSTASY** IS GONNA BE ON THE RECORD TOO.

I **KNOW** Y'ALL WON'T MIND.

BET!

IT TAKES A **FEW** DAYS, BUT **JALIL** AND **ECSTASY** COME UP WITH THE LYRICS FOR **MAGIC'S WAND** , A SONG OBVIOUSLY INSPIRED BY **HIP HOP'S** RADIO CHAMPION.

I HEARD OF A **HEART ATTACK** OR A **BIG MAC ATTACK** BUT WHAT'S A **RAP ATTACK** ?

JIVE IS HAPPY ENOUGH WITH SALES THAT THEY PURSUE NURTURING JALIL AND ECSTASY AS A GROUP. THE **COMPANY** COMES UP WITH THE NAME **HOUDINI** AS AN HOMAGE TO **MR. MAGIC**.

WHODINI IS MORE FLYER!

ANOTHER PERSON INTERESTED IN BUILDING **WHODINI** AS A GROUP IS **RUSSELL SIMMONS**, WHO HAS BEGUN **CULTIVATING** MORE TALENT TO PROMOTE UNDER HIS UMBRELLA, **RUSH MANAGEMENT**.

KURTIS BLOW

LARRY SMITH

YO, THAT **PLANET ROCK** REKKID ITH **NERVITH**.

SPYDER D

EASY D

JIMMY SPICER

RUN

SUGAR HILL RECORDS, STILL LOOKING FOR THEIR NEXT BIG HIT, BRAINSTORMS THAT A PRODUCED-IN-STUDIO BATTLE RECORD MIGHT CAPTURE PEOPLE'S ATTENTION. THE FURIOUS FIVE MEETS THE SUGARHILL GANG'S SHOWDOWN SPRINGS FROM THIS IDEA. THIS RECORD ISN'T PRODUCED BY SUGAR HILL'S USUAL STUDIO MUSICIANS, BUT BY TWO ECCENTRIC BLOOD BROTHERS MICHAEL AND LARRY JOHNSON.

THE BOSTONIAN BROTHERS HAVE THEIR OWN GROUP, THE JONZUN CREW, A MIX BETWEEN FUNK, HIP HOP, AND ELECTRO. THEY EVEN HAVE A REGIONAL HIT ON THEIR OWN LABEL.

THE JONZUN CREW

B
Boston International Records

STEREO
BIR 682 B
Time: 6:38
Boston Int'l
Music/ASCAP

PAK MAN
(LOOK OUT FOR THE OVC)
(M. Jonzun/M. Starr)
Produced by Michael Jonzun/Maurice Starr
Executive Producer: Roscoe Gorham
Recorded at Boston Intl. Records Studio
Engineered by: M. Jonzun
Asst. Engrs: S. Burton, E. Pettway & M. Starr

TOMMY BOY RECORDS HAS GREAT SUCCESS WITH PLANET ROCK, WHICH GIVES THEM MONEY TO PLAY WITH, BUT THEY DON'T HAVE MUCH OF A PLAN. CEO TOM SILVERMAN THINKS THE JONZUN CREW ARE CLOSE ENOUGH TO BAMBAATAA AND THE SOUL SONIC FORCE.

TOMMY BOY
THE JONZUN CREW

TB-826 A
Time: 5:59
BPM: 125
© T-Boy Music/ASCAP

PACK JAM
(Look Out For The OVC)
(Vocal)
(M. Jonzun/M. Starr)
Produced By MICHAEL JONZUN/MAURICE STARR
Exec Producers R. GORHAM/T. SILVERMAN
Remix By JOHN "JELLYBEAN" BENITEZ
Engineered By M. JONZUN
NY 10028

TOMMY BOY ALSO COMMISSIONS SEVERAL MORE JONZUN CREW SINGLES, INCLUDING SPACE IS THE PLACE, SPACE COWBOY, AND WE ARE THE JONZUN CREW. IN 1983, TOMMY BOY DECIDES TO START MAKING FULL-LENGTH ALBUMS, AND LOST IN SPACE BY THE JONZUNS IS THEIR FIRST.

LARRY JOHNSON, NOW KNOWN AS MAURICE STARR OF THE JONZUN CREW ISN'T HAPPY WITH HIS RECORDING CAREER. HE HOLDS A TALENT SHOW IN BOSTON AND PROMISES A $500 CASH PRIZE AND RECORDING DEMO CONTRACT. HE ACTUALLY DECIDES THE KIDS WHO PLACED SECOND ARE MOST INTERESTING. WITH THE JACKSON 5 IN MIND, HE CALLS THE GROUP NEW EDITION.

ABC EASY AS 1-2-3!

STARR'S ASSOCIATION WITH TOMMY BOY PUTS HIM IN PROXIMITY TO THE PLANET ROCK PRODUCER ARTHUR BAKER, WHO HAS STARTED HIS OWN LABEL, STREETWISE RECORDS. NEW EDITION'S FIRST SINGLE, CANDY GIRL, IS A HIT FOR THE COMPANY.

CANDY GIRL! YOU ARE MY WORLD!!

NEW EDITION TOURS FOR MONTHS AND MONTHS TO PROMOTE THEIR BIG HIT. IT'S SAID THAT WHEN THEY FINALLY GET OFF THE ROAD AND GO HOME EACH MEMBER OF THE GROUP MAKES A PROFIT OF...

$1.87?

ONCE MAJOR LABEL INTEREST IS ESTABLISHED NEW EDITION QUICKLY DROPS MAURICE STARR.

IF I TAKE THIS JACKSON 5 FORMULA AND FIND A HANDFUL OF WHITE BOYS TO FILL THE ROLES I MIGHT COULD MAKE A ZILLION.

...AND THAT'S JUST WHAT STARR SETS TO DO. AFTER AUDITIONING HUNDREDS OF WHITE TEENAGE MALES, HE FINALLY NOTICES DONALD EDMOND WAHLBERG JR. AND HIS KID BROTHER MARKY BECAUSE OF THEIR RAP SKILLS.

DONNY, THE SHIT'S SOFT!

IN 1984, STARR'S METICULOUS MANUFACTURING PROCESS RESULTS IN A GROUP CALLED NEW KIDS ON THE BLOCK. YOU MAY HAVE HEARD OF THEM.

DURING THIS TIME MAURICE STARR ADOPTS A NEW PERSONA.

WHY'M I THE GENERAL?

'CAUSE I'M THE MAN THAT GET THINGS DONE.

RUSSELL SIMMONS FINDS THAT HE HAS A KNACK FOR **MANAGEMENT** AND **PRODUCTION** WHEN IT COMES TO THE **HIP HOP** GAME. BEING ONE OF THE **FIRST** PROMOTERS OUT OF THE GATE, HE HAS AN INTIMATE KNOWLEDGE OF ALL THESE BACK-END **BUSINESS** COMPONENTS.

HIS PALS **JB MOORE** AND **ROCKY FORD**, THE PRODUCERS OF **CHRISTMAS RAPPIN'**, START A RECORD LABEL OF THEIR OWN CALLED **PREP STREET**. RUSSELL RUNS HIS "**RUSH TOWN MANAGEMENT**" AFFAIRS FROM AN OFFICE WITHIN THEIR SPACE. RUSS DEEMS PREP STREET A GOOD FIT FOR **LARRY SMITH'S** BAND **ORANGE KRUSH** TO RELEASE THEIR SINGLE, **ACTION**.

FOR **MERCURY RECORDS** RUSSELL'S GOLDEN GOOSE, **KURTIS BLOW**, MAKES A JOINT CALLED "**TOUGH**" IN 1982, BUT THEY ALSO TRY AND SEE IF THEY CAN TURN KURTIS INTO AN **R AND B** SUCCESS WITH THE SINGLE **DAYDREAMIN'**.

I'M OUTTA HIGH SCHOOL NOW, **BIG BRUTHA**...

YOU GONNA PUT ME AN' D ON **REKKIDS** NOW, OR WHAT?

DJ RUN

EASY D

DJ JAZZY JASE

...BUT THEN AGAIN... IT'S JUS' MY '**MAGINATION**. BEING CLOSE TO YOU WAS SUCH A SWEET **SENSATION**...

... THEN WE HAD TO HAVE... THAT TURRIBLE **CONFRONTATION**... NOW ALL I CAN DO.. TO HELP THIS **SITCH-YOU-AY-SHUUUUUUUUUN**! ♪

THOSE RECORDS AREN'T **NEARLY** AS BIG AS **THE BREAKS** FOR KURTIS BLOW AND MERCURY RECORDS, BUT RUSSELL'S GOOD STANDING WITH THE COMPANY **ENCOURAGES** THE LABEL TO GIVE HIS ARTIST **JIMMY SPICER** A SHOT WITH HIS **ECLECTIC** 12-INCH, **THE BUBBLE BUNCH**.

IN A MAJOR COUP, THE INSANELY POPULAR **PROFILE RECORDS** ALL STARS, **DR. JECKYLL AND MR. HYDE**, ENTRUST THEIR NEW CAREER WITH **RUSSELL "RUSH".** THEIR NEXT RELEASE, **THE CHALLENGE**, DOESN'T QUITE HIT THE MARK, HOWEVER.

AN' IF THEY WASN'T EATIN' DINNER...

...THEY WAS EATIN' **LUNCH** !!!

WE'RE SO NASTY. WE'D LOVE TO TURN YOU **OUT**!

ON THE **DOWN-STROKE** WE NEVER **JOKE**. WE'LL MAKE YOU SCREAM AN' **SHOUT**!

LIKE A DURACELL HE'LL ENERGIZE

READY AND WILLING TO SATISFY

1982 IS A PERIOD OF TRANSITION FOR THE **TREACHEROUS THREE**. AFTER 5 WELL-RECEIVED SINGLES FOR **BOBBY ROBINSON'S ENJOY RECORDS** AND **NOT** HAVING MUCH MONEY TO SHOW FOR IT, THE **GROUP** HEADS OVER TO SUGAR HILL, FOLLOWING THE SAME PATH AS OTHER FORMER ENJOY GROUPS LIKE **GRANDMASTER FLASH** AND **THE FUNKY FOUR**.

KOOL MOE DEE

SPECIAL K

NO MO' CASH, NO MO' REKKIDS.

L A SUNSHINE

THEIR **FIRST** SINGLE FOR **SUGAR HILL** KEEPS WITHIN THE HIP HOP TRADITION OF REMAKING A **CURRENT** HIT WITH THEIR SONG **WHIP IT**, WHICH DIRECTLY PULLS FROM **DAZZ BAND'S LET IT WHIP**.

WHIP... WHIP... WHIP...

THIS DAZZ BAND JAM IS SUCH A **NO-BRAINER** THAT, **SIMULTANEOUSLY**, THE **DISCO FOUR** DO A VERSION FOR **PROFILE** CALLED **WHIP RAP**.

MUSIC... MUSIC... MUSIC...

PREVIOUSLY, THE DISCO FOUR WERE **ALSO** ON ENJOY RECORDS WITH SINGLES LIKE **MOVE TO THE GROOVE** AND **COUNTRY ROCK AND RAP**.

BOBBY ROBINSON'S **SON'S** IN THE **MUTHA FUCKIN'** GROUP AN' WE **STILL** AIN'T GETTIN' **NO** MONEY!

ORIGINAL MATERIAL ISN'T QUITE A **PRIORITY** FOR SUGAR HILL. THE NEXT RE-LEASE FOR THE TREACHEROUS THREE IS AN INTERPRETATION OF THE **POINTER SISTERS** CLASSIC **YES WE CAN-CAN**.

TELL ME **KOOL MOE DEE** CAN...

YOU KNOW I **CAN-CAN!**

FOR THE TREMENDOUSLY TALENTED TREACHEROUS THREE, CREATING CONTEMPORARY RAP COVERS ISN'T THE LEAST BIT FULFILLING.

WE DON'T SEEM TO BE MEETING THEM ENDS, **MOE**.

COOL ON OUT, **SUNSHINE**. THINGS WILL PAY OFF IN THE **END**.

SUGAR HILL HOUSE MUSICIAN **DUKE BOOTEE** WOULD **NEVER** BE ABLE TO PITCH THIS SONG IDEA **VERBALLY** TO THE LABEL. THE STYLE AND PREMISE IS TOO DIVORCED FROM WHAT'S BEING DONE WITH **RAP**.

BROKEN GLASS...

...EVERY-WHERE...

TOILING AWAY IN HIS **MOM'S BASEMENT** HE RECORDS A **SCRATCH TRACK** TO MUSIC SO THAT HE CAN CLEARLY COMMUNICATE HIS IDEAS TO **SYLVIA ROBINSON** AT SUGAR HILL.

IT'S LIKE A **JUNGLE** SOMETIMES...

...IT MAKES ME WONDER HOW I KEEP FROM GOING UNDER...

SHE ENTHUSIASTICALLY RESPONDS TO HIS QUICK AND DIRTY RE-CORDING OF **IN THE JUNGLE**, BOOTEE'S WORKING TITLE.

DUKE, THIS RECORD COULD BE **BIGGER** THAN **PLANET ROCK**.

WE'LL GET OUR **BEST** PEOPLE TO PERFORM IT!

NO WAY THE **SUGARHILL GANG** HAS THE STREET CRED FOR THESE HEAVY **URBAN** LYRICS. THE **BRONX** FLAVOR OF **GRANDMASTER FLASH AND THE FURIOUS FIVE** ARE THE LOGICAL FIRST CHOICE.

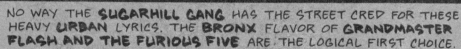

YOU CAN'T **DANCE** TO THIS SHIT!

IT'S TOO **SLOW**.

NO, SYLVIA.

WE'D **KILL** OUR CAREERS.

PEOPLE COME TO OUR JAMS TO FORGET ABOUT THIS KINDA SHIT!!

DUKE BOOTEE'S GOING TO HELP WITH THE VOCALS, BUT IF **YOU** PERFORM THE MAIN LYRICS, **MELVIN**, I THINK WE COULD MAKE YOU A **STAR**.

WHEN **MELLE MEL** AGREES TO PERFORM ON THE RECORD, NOW CALLED **THE MESSAGE**, SYLVIA MAKES MOVES TO GET THE RIGHTS TO ONE OF HIS OLD **SUPERAPPIN'** VERSES TO CLOSE THE SONG OUT.

A CHILD IS BORN WITH NO STATE OF **MIND**...

...**BLIND** TO THE WAYS OF **MAN-KIND**...

ONCE **FLASH** CATCHES WIND THAT MELLE MEL IS DOING THE RECORD, HE TRIES TO GET THE REST OF THE GROUP INVOLVED, BUT THAT SHIP'S SAILED.

BUT **WHY** WOULD YOU **STILL** SAY IT'S A **GRANDMASTER FLASH AND THE FURIOUS FIVE** RECORD IF THE GROUP **AIN'T** ON IT?

SEE, THE **PROBLEM** IS THAT YOU ASK A LOT OF **QUESTIONS**, FLASH-BABY.

FOR THE RECORD, WHEN Y'ALL SIGNED WITH ME I **BOUGHT** THE NAME GRANDMASTER FLASH AND THE FURIOUS FIVE, SO I'LL DO WHAT I FEEL...

DON'T WORRY, THOUGH. I GOT A SPOT FOR Y'ALL ON THE RECORD.

IN HOMAGE TO **STEVIE WONDER'S LIVIN' FOR THE CITY,** FLASH AND CREW CHIME IN AT THE END OF THE RECORD TO CREATE A MOCK STREET SCENE.

WE CAN GO TO THE **FEVER.** CHECK OUT **JUNE-BUG.**

THE MESSAGE TESTS FAVORABLY IN RECORD SHOPS AROUND **NEW YORK.** THEY TRY THE **VINYL** OUT AT **DISCO FEVER** TOO. DESPITE THE HEAVY LYRICAL CONTENT AND **SLOWER** PACE, THE FUNKY RHYTHM CAN KEEP PEOPLE DANCING EVEN WHEN PLAYED AFTER **PLANET ROCK.**

THE MUSIC ROPES YOU IN, BUT THE **BITING** VERSES ARE IMMEDIATELY RELATABLE TO ALMOST ANYONE **BELOW** A CERTAIN TAX BRACKET DURING **RONALD REAGAN'S** REIGN.

DON'T PUSH **ME**... 'CAUSE I'M CLOSE TO THE... **EDGE**...

...I'M TRYIN' **NOT** TO LOSE MY **HEAD**...

THE MESSAGE HITS **4TH** ON THE **BILLBOARD** CHART, THE SAME POSITION ONCE HELD BY PLANET ROCK. IT **DOESN'T** QUITE SELL AS MANY RECORDS AS THE **BAMBAATAA** JOINT, BUT IT IS THE **FIFTH** CERTIFIED **GOLD** RAP SINGLE AND PROVES THAT THE MUSIC CAN BE DEEPER AND MORE **SOCIALLY CONSCIOUS** THAN THE STANDARD **PARTY JAMS** DU JOUR.

SCORPIO — KID CREOLE — COWBOY — EASY MIKE* — MELLE MEL — RAHIEM — FLASH

* EASY MIKE IS GRANDMASTER FLASH'S ASSISTANT. —ED

OH YEAH, THERE IS A **MUSIC VIDEO** TOO. **DUKE BOOTEE** DOESN'T GET TO FILM HIS VERSES WITH **MELLE MEL** THOUGH. **RAHIEM** LIP SYNCS HIS LINES. DUKE DOESN'T MIND MUCH EITHER. IT'S **NOT** LIKE **MTV** WOULD CONSIDER AIRING THE VIDEO ANYTIME SOON.

WHAT WE'RE GONNA DO RIGHT HERE IS GO BACK... **WAY BACK**... BACK INTO TIME.. A LITTLE BEFORE **1979**... IN THE CITY... CITY OF **COMPTON**...

LOWRIDER CULTURE HAS GROWN PRETTY STRONG IN **LOS ANGELES**, AND **ALONZO WILLIAMS** IS THE KIND OF GUY WHO LIKES TO BE AT THE **FOREFRONT**.

SITTIN' ON **DAYTONS**!

TO DISTINGUISH HIS **CAR CLUB** FROM THE REST HE THROWS A **FUNDRAISER** TO BUY SPECIAL JACKETS FOR HIS **CREW**.

LONZO'S PASSION TURNS TO **DJ**ING PARTIES AFTER HEARING ENOUGH TIMES THAT HIS **DELIVERY** WOULD **PREVENT** HIM FROM EVER BECOMING A **RADIO DISC JOCKEY**.

YETH YETH, Y'ALL...

YA DON'T THTOP...

AS HE BOOKS MORE AND MORE VENUES AROUND TOWN, LONZO'S SUCCESS, POPULARITY, AND STAGE PRESENTATION EXPANDS TO **MYTHIC** PROPORTIONS.

SOON ENOUGH, HIS **OPERATION** REQUIRES MORE HANDS THAN HE HAS AVAILABLE, SO HE CREATES THE **DISCO CONSTRUCTION AND WRECKIN' CRU** TO PROVIDE HELP AT JAMS.

ANDRE MANUEL DECIDES TO JOIN THE CREW OF ROADIES AND ASSISTANTS BECAUSE HE'S INTERESTED IN LEARNING TO DJ HIMSELF.

WHERE SHOULD I PUT THESE RECORDS, **LONZ**?

THIS'LL ALL PAY OFF IN THE END...

LONZO'S BUILDING SUCH A **REPUTATION** THAT EVEN HIS **FATHER** CAN'T HELP BUT NOTICE.

BOY, YOU PAY TOO MUCH TO RENT THESE GYMS AND HALLS...

...LET ME SEE WHAT I CAN DO FOR YOU.

HIS DAD SECURES A **REGULAR** GIG AT A FRIEND'S NIGHT CLUB CALLED **EVE AFTER DARK**, STRATEGICALLY LOCATED IN **L.A. COUNTY**.

BEING IN **L.A. COUNTY**, THE VENUE ISN'T BOUND BY THE 2 A.M. CLOSING ORDINANCES OF **LOS ANGELES** OR **COMPTON**, WHICH MEANS THE PARTY CAN GO ALL NIGHT.

LONZO SETS ROOTS IN THIS **CATBIRD SEAT** AND MAKES **THOUSANDS** OF **DOLLARS** EVERY **WEEK**.

WITH THESE LONGER SESSIONS, WRECKIN' CRU MEMBER **ANDRE MANUEL** HELPS WITH THE DJ DUTIES. INSPIRED BY THE "UNKNOWN COMEDIAN" ON THE GONG SHOW HE ADOPTS THE NAME **UNKNOWN DJ**.

MORE ASSISTANCE ON THE WHEELS COMES FROM A YOUNG **ANTOINE CARRABY**, NICKNAMED **DJ YELLA** BY UNKNOWN DJ AFTER A 1981 TOM TOM CLUB SONG.

UMMM...

HI!

SINCE THE CLUB STAYS OPEN SO LATE, LONZO TRIES TO KEEP THE **RIFF-RAFF** OUT BY INCORPORATING A STRICT **DRESS CODE**.

C'MON **LONZO-MAN**, I KNOW FOR A **FACK** THAT **YELLA** AIN'T 18 EITHER!

Y'ALL GOT TA GIT, NOW.

ANDRE YOUNG CAN'T CONVINCE LONZO THAT HE'S MUSICALLY TALENTED ENOUGH TO BYPASS THE AGE LIMIT FOR ENTRY. HIS **DRUG DEALER** PAL **ERIC WRIGHT'S** SOCIAL STATUS DOESN'T WORK FOR ACCESS EITHER.

EVEN IF Y'ALL WERE OLD ENOUGH I WOULDN'T LETCHALL IN...

...LOOKIN' ALL RAGGEDY AN' SHIT... SHAMEFUL!

FUCK YOU! SYLVESTER THE CAT-SOUNDING **MOTHER FUCKER!!**

BOY, I'LL SQUASH YOU WITH THEETH THTATHY ADAM'TH SHOE'TH...

YO **EAZY**, LETS BREAK OUT. THIS SHIT IS **WEAK**.

BEFORE SETTLING AT EVE AFTER DARK, **LONZO WILLIAMS'** MOBILE DJ CAREER BROUGHT HIM TO PLAY PARTIES PROMOTED BY **ROGER CLAYTON'S** DJ COMPANY CALLED **UNIQUE DREAMS**.

UNIQUE DREAMS DANCES BECOME A DOMINATING FORCE IN **LOS ANGELES**. ROGER CLAYTON CHANGES THE NAME OF HIS CREW TO **UNCLE JAMM'S ARMY** BASED ON THE **FUNKADELIC** SONG **UNCLE JAM**, AND HIS BUSINESS DOESN'T MISS A STEP.

THESE POSTERS IS **EVERYWHERE**. WHY DO YOU THINK GIRLS GET INTO THE JAMS FOR CHEAPER THAN THE BRUTHAS?

YOU AXE STUPID QUESTIONS.

EVER EXPANDING IN THE WAKE OF LONZO'S SEDENTARY POSITION, CLAYTON HOLDS A **CONTEST** TO GROW HIS ROSTER OF **DJ'S**. **EGYPTIAN LOVER** WINS THE HONOR, HANDS DOWN, WITH HIS TRICKS ON THE **PLATTER** AND HIS STYLE, WHICH IS SOMEWHERE BETWEEN **PRINCE** AND **KRAFTWERK**.

THE UNCLE JAMM'S PARTIES FOCUSED ON UPTEMPO **FUNK** MUSIC UNTIL THE **SUGAR HILL** RECORDS FROM THE **EAST COAST** STARTED CREEPING CROSS COUNTRY.

WE ROCK...

AND DON'T STOP...

THE **DANCE CULTURE** IN L.A. IS PROBABLY MORE DOMINANT THAN THE **NEW YORK** COUNTERPARTS IN **HIP HOP**. **ICE T**, HIMSELF, HAS DITCHED THE MOBILE DJ GRIND, BUT COMES TO **UNCLE JAMM'S** EVENTS TO **POP AND LOCK** WITH THE BEST OF 'EM.

ONCE EGYPTIAN LOVER AND CREW DISCOVER ICE'S SKILL AT **STREET RHYMING**, THEY GIVE HIM A CHANCE TO ROCK THE MIC EVEN THOUGH THEIR PARTIES **AREN'T** MC DRIVEN **AT ALL**.

...WHEN MY DOCTOR SPANKED MY BUTT IT WAS ON THE BEAT...

51

ICE CONTINUES TO HONE HIS CRAFT AT **ANY** OPPORTUNITY.

I'M THE **HULA DULA,** THE HO-HOUSE RULER...

HOW WOULD YOU LIKE TO PUT SOME RHYMES DOWN ON WAX WITH ME?

FOOL, IS YOU TRY'NA PLAY ME FOR A **SUCKA?**

FOR WHATEVER REASON, **ICE T** ACTUALLY DOES LEAVE WITH THE MYSTERY MAN ONCE HIS HAIR'S FINISHED. THEY HEAD TO A STUDIO AND RECORD **THE COLDEST RAP** FOR **SATURN RECORDS.**

T DOESN'T HAVE ANY DELUSIONS ABOUT MAKING MONEY IN THE **RAP** GAME. HE'S BUILDING HIS OWN **EMPIRE** IN THE STREETS AND DOESN'T NEED THOSE SORTS OF DISTRACTIONS.

MAKIN' COLD CASH MONEY IN MY SLEEP AIN'T NO THANG.

TURNS OUT SATURN RECORDS OWNS A RECORD SHOP IN TOWN AND THEY PROMINENTLY FEATURE THEIR FRESH **ICE T** RECORD.

YO! THIS GUY HERE LOOKS LIKE **MAD MAX** AN' SHIT!

I'M BUYIN' IT!

THE DJ'S AT THE **RADIO CLUB** HAVE COME TO RELY ON THIS LOCALLY PRODUCED JAM TO GET PEOPLE GROOVING ON THE DANCE FLOOR.

YOU CAN ASK YOUR FATHER, YOUR SISTER, OR **MOTHER...**

...I GOT A ROLLS ROYCE IN EVERY **COLOR...**

CHRIS "THE GLOVE" TAYLOR

IT MAKES SENSE FOR THEM TO TRACK DOWN ICE T TO PERFORM THE COLDEST RAP **LIVE,** BUT IT'S A BATTLE TO GET HIM TO SEE THE POINT.

>GULP< WHY SHOULD I BUST MY **RHYMES** IN A ROOM FULL OF **WHITE PEOPLE?**

WITH TREPIDATION ICE MOVES TO THE STAGE TO RECITE HIS RECORD AND MUCH TO HIS ASTONISHMENT...

...I'M A PLAYA, THAT'S ALL I **KNOW...** ON A SUMMER DAY I PLAY IN THE **SNOW...**

...FROM THE **WOMB** TO THE **TOMB** I RUN MY **GAME...**

...CAUSE I'M COLD AS ICE... AND I SHOW NO **SHAME...**

ICE T BEGINS TO BELIEVE THAT A CAREER IN THE RAP GAME MIGHT NOT BE CRAZY AFTER THIS PERFORMANCE.

ANDRE YOUNG WAS 5 YEARS OLD WHEN HE STARTED PROGRAMMING MUSIC AT HOUSE PARTIES FOR HIS MOM, VERNA. HE MADE NOTE THAT PEOPLE WOULD REALLY GET **CRAZY** WHENEVER A **PARLIAMENT/FUNKADELIC** SONG WOULD PLAY.

ANDRE BECAME **OBSESSED**, LOSING HIMSELF IN MUSIC WHILE GROWING UP IN THE WARZONE OF **COMPTON, CALIFORNIA**. ON HIS 15TH BIRTHDAY, INSTEAD OF A BIKE OR A BASEBALL GLOVE, **DRE'S** MOM GOT HIM...

... A MIXER!

THANKS, MA!

THIS PUSHED HIM FURTHER DOWN THAT RABBIT HOLE. HE'D CONSTANTLY BE IN HIS BEDROOM WITH HIS RECORDS. **CUTTING, SCRATCHING, EXPERIMENTING.**

OFF AND RUNNING IN THE EARLY 80S, DRE IS WELL AWARE OF **HIP HOP** CULTURE ON THE EAST COAST AND TRIES TO IMPLEMENT SOME OF THAT INTO THE COMPTON **BLOCK PARTIES** HE DJS.

IF YOU GONNA **RUIN** THEM REKKIDS YOU BEST DO IT ON BEAT. I'M TRY'NA GIT DOWN WIT' MY **HO**.

WORKING HARD TO PERFECT HIS CRAFT, ANDRE SOON CAN GET MOST ANY CROWD UNDER HIS SPELL.

IN HOPES OF A STEADY INCOME, HIS GOAL IS TO GET A REGULAR SPOT AT LONZO WILLIAMS'S CLUB, **EVE AFTER DARK**, BUT HE'S NEVER EVEN ALLOWED TO STEP FOOT IN THE JOINT.

ARE YOU KIDDIN'? **LONZO'S** MY MAN, DRE.

LET ME TALK TO HIM FOR YA.

DRE'S BIG CHANCE AT **EVE AFTER DARK** COMES ONE NIGHT WHEN ANOTHER DJ **NO-SHOWS**. COMMITTED TO BLOW THE CROWD'S MIND WITH SOME MAGIC HE CONCOCTED IN HIS BEDROOM, ANDRE COMBINES THE INSTRUMENTAL PARTS OF **PLANET ROCK** WITH VOCALS FROM **THE MARVELETTES** CLASSIC...

HEY MR. POSTMAN...

...LOOK AT ME!!!

...DA FUCK!? AIN'T NOBODY DANTHIN'! I'LL **KILL** THAT L'IL **MUTHA**...

LONZO, THIS KID'S INCREDIBLE, MAN.

EVERYBODY ON THE FLOOR IS **MESMERIZED** BY HIM. WHO THE HELL IS HE?

UH...

HE'TH THE NEWETHT MEMBER OF THE **WORLD CLATH WRECKIN' CRU**, NAME'TH **DR. DRE**.

HE PERFORM'TH THURGERY ON DEM REKKIDTH WITH ALL 'AT **CUTTIN'**.

FOR THE 12-HOUR NIGHTS AT EVE AFTER DARK, **LONZO** FASHIONS THE DJ ROSTER LIKE A RADIO STATION OR A PITCHER'S BULLPEN. IF YOU DON'T PERFORM WELL, YOUR **ASS** GETS **REPLACED**.

LONZO WILLIAMS, HIMSELF, WILL FILL ANY ROLE IN THE SLOT. HE CAN **ALWAYS** GET PEOPLE ON THE FLOOR TO **DANCE**.

UNKNOWN DJ HAS THE MOST EXPERIENCE AFTER LONZO, SO HE WORKS THE BIGGER CROWDS.

DJ YELLA AND **DR. DRE** OPEN AND CLOSE EACH EVENING, PLAYING TO MODEST AUDIENCES. THESE BOYS HAVE DUES TO PAY.

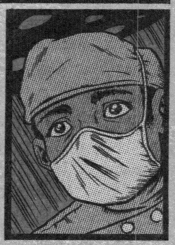

54

ON **LONG ISLAND**, TEENAGE **CARLTON D. RIDENHOUR** IS A SPORTS FAN WITH AN INTEREST IN BECOMING A RADIO ANNOUNCER. WHILE WAITING IN LINE AT THE CROWDED BASKETBALL COURT HE IS NO STRANGER TO **RAP CYPHERS.**

DIP-DIP-DIVE... SO-SOCIALIZE...

YOU **CAN'T** ESCAPE **HIP HOP** IN THE LATE 70s/EARLY 80s. THERE ARE A LOT OF **3RD-RATE** JAMS WITH LOTS OF **C-LEVEL** TALENT.

THESE WACK MC'S AIN'T INSPIRING THE GIRLIES TO DANCE AT ALL.

THE VOICES OF THESE SOFT MC'S COULDN'T PENETRATE THE CROWD WITH WEAK SOUND EQUIPMENT, BUT WHEN **CARLTON** WOULD GRAB THE MIC IN **FRUSTRATION...**

EMCEE CHUCKIE D...

...IN THE PLACE TO BE...

TWO OF THE MORE ENTERPRISING DJ'S ON THE LONG ISLAND SCENE, **HANK SHOCKLEE** AND HIS BROTHER, **WIZARD K-JEE**, BEGIN TO INCORPORATE THE VOCAL POWERS OF **MC CHUCKIE D** INTO THEIR PARTIES.

IF IT'S NOT IN THE CARDS FOR **CHUCK** TO BECOME A SPORTS BROADCASTER, HIS PLAN B IS IN **GRAPHIC DESIGN**. HE PUTS HIS AESTHETIC TASTE AND ABILITY TO GOOD USE BY COMING UP WITH A COOL LOGO FOR HIS NEW CREW, WHICH ALSO INCLUDES **DJ GRIFF.**

SPECTRUM CITY

SPECTRUM CITY QUICKLY BECOMES THE **PREMIERE** GROUP DOING HIP HOP PARTIES ON **LONG ISLAND...**

CHECK! ONE, TWO...

GIT THE FUCK OFF!

THEIR SPEAKERS AREN'T INFERIOR. **CHUCK D'S** RAP IS AS **POWERFUL** AS EVER, BUT...

MY NAME IS MC CHUC D WITH...

Y'ALL A BUNCHA JOKES

...IT'S JUST THAT **MELLE MEL** DOESN'T WANT THE YOUNGSTERS TO GET TOO FULL OF THEMSELVES BEFORE **PAYING DUES** AND HE DOESN'T NEED A **MICROPHONE** TO EXPRESS HIMSELF OVER THE CROWD...

BITCH

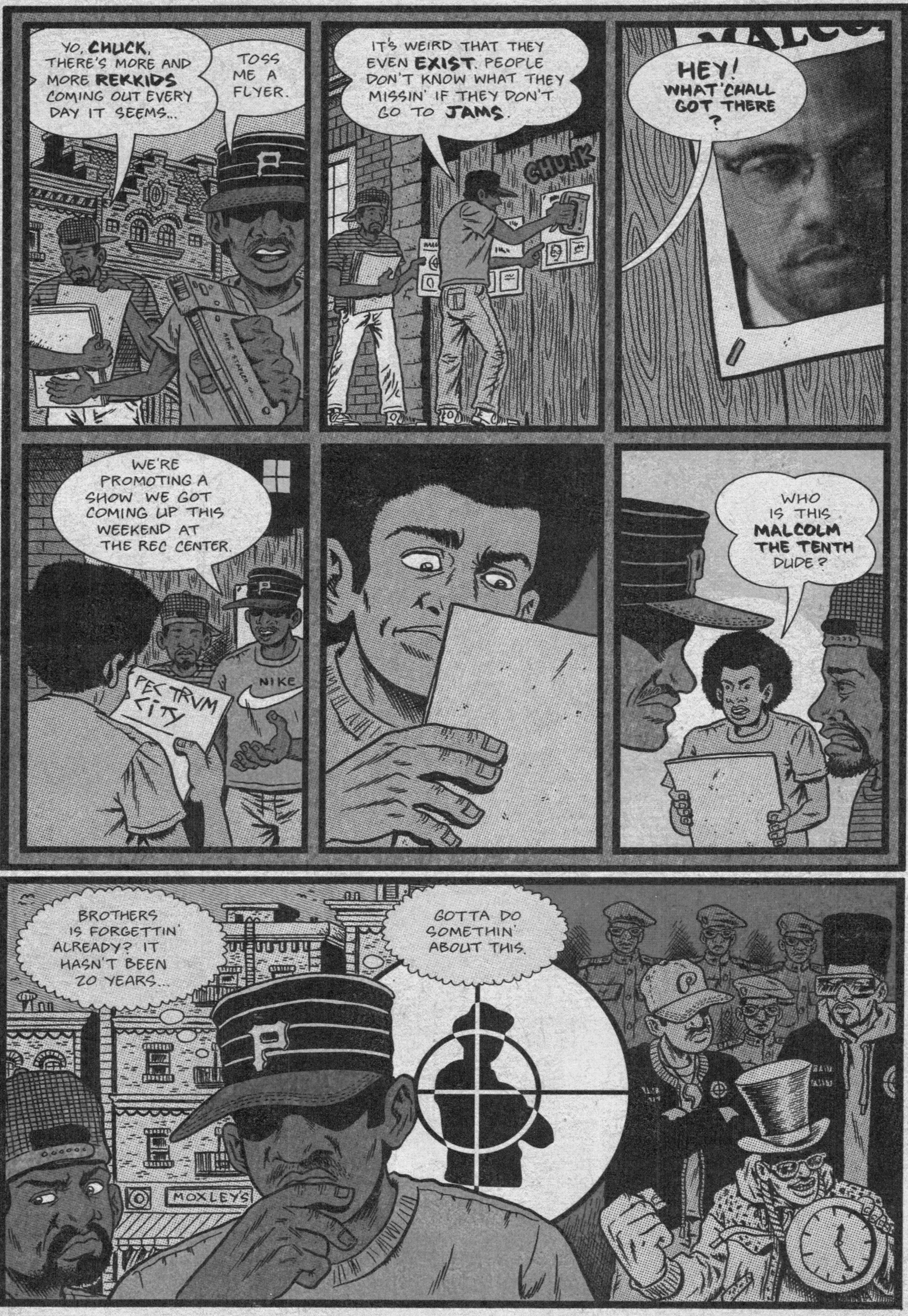
YO, CHUCK, THERE'S MORE AND MORE REKKIDS COMING OUT EVERY DAY IT SEEMS...
TOSS ME A FLYER.
IT'S WEIRD THAT THEY EVEN EXIST. PEOPLE DON'T KNOW WHAT THEY MISSIN' IF THEY DON'T GO TO JAMS.
CHUNK
HEY! WHAT'CHALL GOT THERE?
WE'RE PROMOTING A SHOW WE GOT COMING UP THIS WEEKEND AT THE REC CENTER.
PEC TRVM CITY
NIKE
WHO IS THIS MALCOLM THE TENTH DUDE?
BROTHERS IS FORGETTIN' ALREADY? IT HASN'T BEEN 20 YEARS...
GOTTA DO SOMETHIN' ABOUT THIS.
MOXLEYS

FOR **SUGAR HILL** RECORDS, **GRANDMASTER FLASH AND THE FURIOUS FIVE'S** SINGLE **THE MESSAGE** GOES **GOLD** IN ITS FIRST 21 DAYS AND **PLATINUM** IN 41.

THINK THEY GOT ANY **TJ SWANN** OVER HERE?

FOO' THESE PEOPLE INVENTED **WINE**!

Y'ALL **STUPID**!

RECOGNIZING THAT THE SUCCESS OF THE MESSAGE MAY LIE WITH THE TANDEM OF **MELLE MEL** AND **DUKE BOOTEE**, SUGAR HILL PROMPTS THEM TO CREATE AND PERFORM THE RECORD **MESSAGE II (SURVIVAL)**.

ONLY THE **STRONG** CAN SURVIVE...

EVEN THOUGH THE ENTIRE GROUP DIDN'T PUT EITHER **MESSAGE** RECORD TOGETHER, THEY ALL NONETHELESS ARE GUESTS ON THE **MAY 21, 1983,** EPISODE OF **SOUL TRAIN**, ACTING AS BACK-UP DANCERS WHILE **MELLE MEL** ROCKS THE HOUSE.

NEXT UP, **GRANDMASTER FLASH AND THE FURIOUS FIVE** IS THE NAME ON THE LABEL FOR THEIR NEW SONG, **NEW YORK NEW YORK**, BUT THE RECORD IS MOSTLY **MEL** AND **DUKE** ONCE AGAIN.

...**FUCKIN' BULLSHIT**!

ON TOP OF THIS, SUGAR HILL HASN'T BEEN KEEPING UP WITH **ROYALTY** PAYMENTS TO FLASH, FORCING HIM TO TAKE THE LABEL TO COURT FOR **$5 MILLION** IN BACK PAY.

FLASH COMES OUT OF THE CASE WITH **NOTHING** BUT A RULING THAT HE'S **ALLOWED** TO KEEP HIS NAME IF HE SO CHOOSES TO RECORD FOR ANOTHER COMPANY.

57

THE **LITIGATION** CREATES A FAULT BETWEEN THE GROUP, CAUSING MEMBERS TO CHOOSE SIDES. BREAKING FROM SUGAR HILL, **GRANDMASTER FLASH AND THE FURIOUS FIVE** CONSISTS OF **KID CREOLE** AND **RAHIEM** FROM THE ORIGINAL CREW AND ADDS **LORD LAVON**, **MR. BROADWAY**, AND **LARRY LOVE** TO BALANCE THE ROSTER.

WE'RE GRANDMASTER FLASH! WE'RE GIVING YOU A BLAST OF CLASS! AND IF YOU WANNA KNOW WHY WE'RE ON TOP OF THE PILE... 'CAUSE WE GOT STYLE...

AT SUGAR HILL, AS AN **OBVIOUS** DIG AT FLASH, **GRANDMASTER MELLE MEL AND THE FURIOUS FIVE** INCLUDES **MR. NESS/SCORPIO** AND **KEITH COWBOY** FROM THE CLASSIC GROUP AND ROUNDS OUT THE NEW ORGANIZATION WITH **KING LOU**, **KAMI KAZE**, **TOMMY GUNN**, AND **DJ EZ MIKE** ON THE TURNTABLES.

RAAH!!

58

WITH THE LOSS OF **GRANDMASTER FLASH**, **SUGAR HILL RECORDS** MOVES FORWARD WITH WHAT THEY'VE DONE FROM THE START: MAKING RAP RECORDS USING **FAMILIAR** MUSIC. THE **TREACHEROUS THREE** STEP UP TO BAT WITH **ACTION**, BORROWING FROM THE **RUSSELL SIMMONS**, MANAGED GROUP, **ORANGE KRUSH**.

'CUZ IT'S THE SOUND OF THE **DRUM** THAT MAKES YOU **COME**...

'CUZ IT'S THE SOUND OF THE **DRUM** THAT MAKES YOU **COME**...

'CUZ IT'S THE SOUND OF THE **DRUM** THAT MAKES YOU **COME**...

LARRY SMITH, THE LEADER OF **ORANGE KRUSH**...

THEY RIPPED OFF OUR DRUMS **WHOLESALE**!!

1982 IS THE YEAR **RUN**, **D**, AND **JAY** FINALLY GET OUT OF HIGH SCHOOL.

JOSEPH "**DJ RUN**" SIMMONS HEADS TO **LAGUARDIA COMMUNITY COLLEGE** TO BECOME A **MORTICIAN**.

IF PEOPLE GONNA KEEP DYIN' ALL DAY, MIGHT AS WELL TRY AN' MAKE SOME EN'S.

DARRYL "**D THE MC**" McDANIELS ENROLLS AT **ST. JOHNS UNIVERSITY** FOR BUSINESS.

WANNA KNOW GOOD ECONOMICS? COKE COSTS LIKE $25 A BLAST, RIGHT?

BUT, THIS **OLDE E** ONLY COS' A BUCK FITTY-FIVE.

AFTER GETTING HIS **G.E.D.**, JASON "**JAZZY JASE**" MIZELL BECOMES A STUDENT AT **QUEENS COLLEGE**.

THINK I'D GET THIS JOB IF I WAS DRESSED LIKE YOU, SONNY?

I'M NOT NO "SONNY" NOW, PROFESSOR!

BIG BROTHER RUSSELL SIMMONS HAS NOT BEEN LOOKING FORWARD TO THIS.

WHEN WE GONNA MAKE **REKKIDS** TOGETHER, **RUSS**? WHEN YOU GONNA PUT ME ON?

GO GET A MATHTERTH DEGREE THO YOU HAVE THUMTHIN' TO FALL BACK ON!

LARRY SMITH AND ORANGE KRUSH HAVE **REVENGE** ON THEIR MINDS...

LET'S MAKE A **RAP** RECORD!

BEAT THEM AT THEY OWN GAME!!

TREVOR GALE, THE DRUMMER, ALREADY HAS SOME RHYMES AND RHYTHMS READY TO GO WHEN THEY APPROACH **RUSSELL**.

IT'TH CALLED **THTREET KID** ?

I KNOW JUTH THE KID TO PERFORM IT!

RUSSELL OFFERS HIS KID BROTHER UP FOR NO REASON BUT TO GET BOTH PARTIES OFF HIS BACK SO THAT HE CAN SPEND MORE TIME ON HIS BREADWINNER **KURTIS BLOW**.

I WENT TO **HOLLIS AVE** JUST TO SEE WHO'S **THERE**...

PEOPLE JUDGE US BY HOW WE LOOK AND BY WHAT WE **WEAR**...

MY MAN, **DARRYL MACK**, THINKS IT'S ALL A **JOKE**...

BUT ME, MYSELF, I THINK IT'S **WACK** 'CUZ I'M A COOL-OUT **FOLK**...

HE'S A **BEAST**, RUSH!

THE **STREET KID** DEMO DOESN'T GET PICKED UP BY ANY MAJOR RECORD LABELS AND IS, UNFORTUNATELY, LOST TO THE AGES.

RUSSELL, I'M TELLIN' YOU, MAN! MAKE A REKKID WIT' ME AN' D TOGETHER! HE'S THE **BEST** RAPPER OUT!

YOU'RE **NUT'TH**! D'TH RHYME'TH ITH TOO **AGGRETHIVE**. IT'TH UNCOMMERCIAL!

SOME OTHER NOTEWORTHY HITS OF 1982

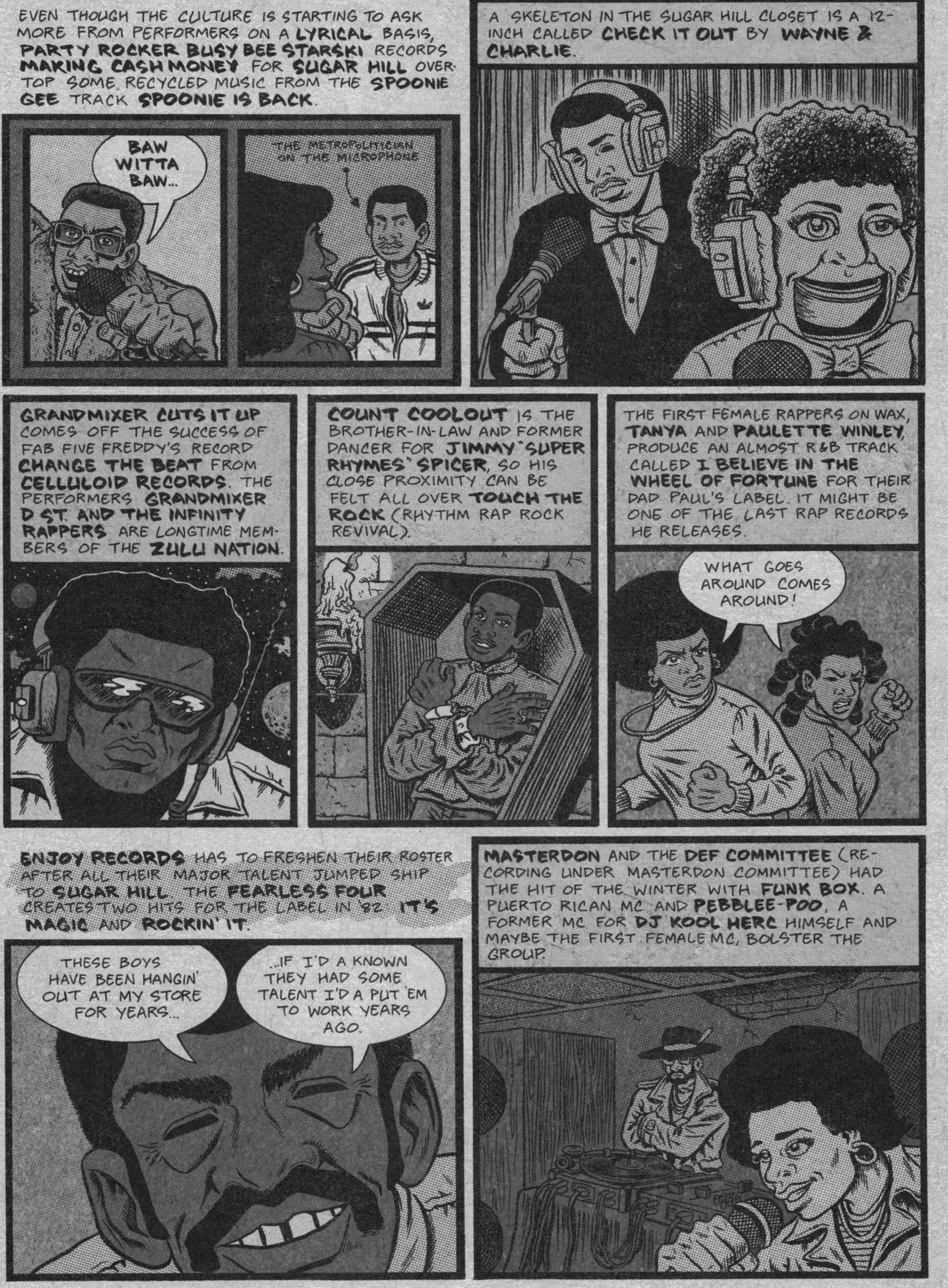
EVEN THOUGH THE CULTURE IS STARTING TO ASK MORE FROM PERFORMERS ON A LYRICAL BASIS, PARTY ROCKER BUSY BEE STARSKI RECORDS MAKING CASH MONEY FOR SUGAR HILL OVER-TOP SOME RECYCLED MUSIC FROM THE SPOONIE GEE TRACK SPOONIE IS BACK.
BAW WITTA BAW...
THE METROPOLITICIAN ON THE MICROPHONE
A SKELETON IN THE SUGAR HILL CLOSET IS A 12-INCH CALLED CHECK IT OUT BY WAYNE & CHARLIE.
GRANDMIXER CUTS IT UP COMES OFF THE SUCCESS OF FAB FIVE FREDDY'S RECORD CHANGE THE BEAT FROM CELLULOID RECORDS. THE PERFORMERS GRANDMIXER D.ST. AND THE INFINITY RAPPERS ARE LONGTIME MEMBERS OF THE ZULU NATION.
COUNT COOLOUT IS THE BROTHER-IN-LAW AND FORMER DANCER FOR JIMMY "SUPER RHYMES" SPICER, SO HIS CLOSE PROXIMITY CAN BE FELT ALL OVER TOUCH THE ROCK (RHYTHM RAP ROCK REVIVAL).
THE FIRST FEMALE RAPPERS ON WAX, TANYA AND PAULETTE WINLEY, PRODUCE AN ALMOST R&B TRACK CALLED I BELIEVE IN THE WHEEL OF FORTUNE FOR THEIR DAD PAUL'S LABEL. IT MIGHT BE ONE OF THE LAST RAP RECORDS HE RELEASES.
WHAT GOES AROUND COMES AROUND!
ENJOY RECORDS HAS TO FRESHEN THEIR ROSTER AFTER ALL THEIR MAJOR TALENT JUMPED SHIP TO SUGAR HILL. THE FEARLESS FOUR CREATES TWO HITS FOR THE LABEL IN '82: IT'S MAGIC AND ROCKIN' IT.
THESE BOYS HAVE BEEN HANGIN' OUT AT MY STORE FOR YEARS...
...IF I'D A KNOWN THEY HAD SOME TALENT I'D A PUT 'EM TO WORK YEARS AGO.
MASTERDON AND THE DEF COMMITTEE (RECORDING UNDER MASTERDON COMMITTEE) HAD THE HIT OF THE WINTER WITH FUNK BOX. A PUERTO RICAN MC AND PEBBLEE-POO, A FORMER MC FOR DJ KOOL HERC HIMSELF AND MAYBE THE FIRST FEMALE MC, BOLSTER THE GROUP.

KOOL KYLE THE STARCHILD RECORDS A SONG CALLED **GETTING OVER** THAT VERY MUCH FEELS INSPIRED BY GRANDMASTER FLASH AND THE FURIOUS FIVE'S **THE MESSAGE**.

WHEELIN' DEALIN' HOMEBOY'S STEALIN'...

...TRYIN' TO GET A BUCK...

KYLE PLAYS A ROLE IN THE FILMING OF **NEW YORK BEAT MOVIE**, A FLICK SPEARHEADED BY SOME FOLKS FROM **GLENN O'BRIEN'S TV PARTY**.

...KLAUS NOMI, ONE OF THE FINEST PASTRY CHEFS IN **NEW YORK**!

IN FACT, THE FILM IS WRITTEN BY GLENN AND REVOLVES AROUND HIS ARTIST PAL **JEAN-MICHEL BASQUIAT**.

YOU WROTE ON MY VAN! I'M GONNA GET YOU, PUNK!

MORE TV PARTY/ART SCENE FIXTURES ARE INCLUDED ON SCREEN LIKE, **DEBBIE HARRY, MICHAEL HOLMAN**, A YOUNG **VINCE GALLO, LEE QUINONES**, AND **FAB FIVE FREDDY**.

WHO ARE YOU? HENRY GODZILLA?

RIGHT AFTER THE SCENE WHERE BASQUIAT BUMPS INTO LEE AND FAB, **KOOL KYLE** IS THE EMCEE IN THE PARTY RAPPING OVER BLONDIE'S **RAPTURE**.

THE FILM, HOWEVER, IS SHELVED FOR **20 YEARS** DUE TO FINANCIAL ISSUES BUT EVENTUALLY PREMIERES AT THE 2000 CANNES FILM FESTIVAL UNDER THE TITLE **DOWNTOWN 81**. 3 YEARS AFTER THAT KYLE DISCOVERS THE FILM'S RELEASE.

ARE YOU **KOOL KYLE**?

I'VE LITERALLY BEEN LOOKING ALL OVER THE WORLD FOR YOU.

?

WHEN WE FINALLY RESCUED THE NEGATIVES THE VOICE TRACKS WERE COMPLETELY DESTROYED.

SINCE I COULDN'T FIND YOU I NEEDED TO HAVE ANOTHER RAPPER OVERDUB THE VOCALS.

WHO?

"MELLE MEL"

EIGHTY-ONE SCHOLARSHIPS

TO EIGHTY-ONE SCHOOLS

LATE ON **107.5 WBLS** EVERY WEEKEND, **MR. MAGIC** AND **DJ JUNEBUG** ARE RELENTLESS ABOUT PROGRAMMING THEIR **RAP** SHOW TO THE HIP HOPPERS OF **NEW YORK CITY**.

ON THE **BROADCAST** THEY NEVER MISS AN OPPORTUNITY TO MENTION THAT EVERY OTHER NIGHT OF THE WEEK THEY CAN BE FOUND AT THE **DISCO FEVER** HOLDING COURT. JUNEBUG'S **INCOME** AND **REPUTATION** ARE ALSO ON THE STEADY RISE BY HIS WORKING TWO JOBS IN TANDEM AT THE FEVER.

CHEAPER THAN GOING TO **THE FEVER**...

:Sniff: WAIT'LL YOU HEAR THIS FRESH RAP WE WORKIN' ON. IT'S KINDA INSPIRED BY YOU...

WE GOT THIS **LIQUID LIQUID** BEAT UNDERNEATH IT. SHIT'S **BUTTER**. :sniff:

SAL ABBATIELLO, THE OWNER OF THE DISCO FEVER, COMES TO THE **REALIZATION**...

SWEET G, ARE YOU FUCKED UP TOO? DON'T THINK THERE'S **ONE** GUY THAT WORK HERE WHO **ISN'T** SKIED UP!

YOU KIDDIN'? AIN'T ONE PERSON IN THE WHOLE BUILDIN' WHO DON'T GOT THEY **NOSE OPEN**.

EARLY ONE NIGHT, **SWEET G**, THE MANAGER AND HOUSE EMCEE AT THE FEVER, AND **MR. MAGIC** HAVE PLANS TO CHECK OUT A MOVIE WITH **JUNEBUG**.

DID YOU KNOW **ROCK STEADY** GOT HIRED TO BE IN THE **FLICK**?

'BUG HASN'T PICKED UP THE PHONE IN **DAYS**. THIS AIN'T LIKE 'IM...

LIKE MANY CRIMES IN THE 'HOOD, **NOBODY** IS VOLUNTEERING **ANY** INFORMATION ABOUT THE WHO'S AND WHY'S JUNEBUG WAS **KILLED**. THE **COPS** CHALK IT UP AS **JUST ANOTHER DRUG-RELATED HOMICIDE**.

PARLAYING HIS SUCCESS FROM **PLANET ROCK** AND OTHER HITS, PRODUCER **ARTHUR BAKER** SETS UP SHOP AT **UNIQUE STUDIOS** AND DECKS IT OUT WITH STATE-OF-THE-ART EQUIPMENT. HIS **GOAL** FOR TODAY: TO FIGURE OUT HIS WAY AROUND HIS LATEST $25,000 PURCHASE, THE **FAIRLIGHT COMPUTER**.

MARLON, DID YOU TOUCH MY SETTINGS AGAIN?

HUH?

INTERN **MARLON WILLIAMS** COULD BE CONSIDERED AN **ENTHUSIASTIC** STUDENT, TO SAY THE LEAST.

NAW, YOU **CRAZY**, ART.

IN HIS FREE TIME MARLON USES THE FACILITIES TO MAKE HIGH-QUALITY **MIX TAPES** WHICH ARE POPULAR IN HIS NATIVE **QUEENS**.

I CAN'T LIVE WITHOUT MY RADIO.

HE DOESN'T HAVE MUCH TIME TO HIMSELF BECAUSE HE ALSO INTERNS AT RADIO STATION **WBLS**.

ONE COFFEE WITH CREAM AN' TWO SUGARS...

...ONE **BLACK**...

YOU'RE ONE HELL OF A MAN, **MARLEY**.

IT DOESN'T TAKE LONG FOR **MR. MAGIC** TO DISCOVER THE KID.

YOU GONNA LET ME PLAY A TAPE ON THE SHOW?

WHY WOULD I DO THAT?

'CAUSE 2.5 MILLION PEOPLE LISTEN TO ME.

SOUND GOOD TO ME.

MARLEY FILLS THE VOID **JUNEBUG** LEFT, AND HE AND MR. MAGIC FIND THAT THEY'RE A GOOD MATCH AS THEY JOIN FORCES TO **BROADCAST EVERY SATURDAY**...

RAP ATTACK

MITHTER MAGIC...

...MARLEY MARL...

BAD MUH FUGGA'TH...

LIGHTS OUT, CHRISTOPHER!!!

AS **1983** COMES ALONG, **TOMMY BOY RECORDS** MAKES SURE TO PUT AFRIKA BAMBAATAA & THE **SOUL SONIC FORCE** TO WORK ON THE HEELS OF THEIR BREAKOUT HIT **PLANET ROCK**.

LOOKING FOR THE PERFECT BEAT...

I'M AFRIKA BAMBAATAA... I POSSESS THE PERFECT BEAT...

RENEGADES OF FUNK...

RADIO EXECS AT **KISS 98.7** SPRING INTO ACTION TO TRY AND CAPTURE SOME OF **MR. MAGIC'S** AUDIENCE AT **107.5 WBLS.** THE FIRST GUY THEY APPROACH TO HOST A NEW MIX SHOW IS THE "MASTER OF RECORDS" HIMSELF, **AFRIKA BAM-BAATAA.**

I GOT TOO MUCH GOIN' ON BUT I KNOW SOME PEOPLE.

BAM'S FIRST CHOICE FOR THIS OPPORTUNITY IS **AFRIKA ISLAM,** WHO HAS HIS OWN TIME-LEASE PROGRAM ON **WHBI** CALLED **ZULU BEATS.**

HE DIDN'T SHOW UP TO THE STUDIO? I GOT ANOTHER GUY IN MIND. DON'T WORRY ABOUT IT.

DJ JAZZY JAY SOON TAKES THE REINS TO CAPTAIN THE NEW SHOW, AND MR. MAGIC HAS BEEN PREPARING HIMSELF FOR THIS MOMENT.

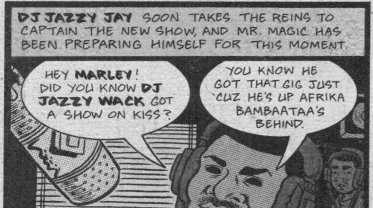

HEY **MARLEY!** DID YOU KNOW **DJ JAZZY WACK** GOT A SHOW ON KISS?

YOU KNOW HE GOT THAT GIG JUST 'CUZ HE'S UP AFRIKA BAMBAATAA'S BEHIND.

SO I **DON'T** GET TO MAKE ANY MONEY, **PLUS** I GOTTA TAKE MAGIC **DISSIN'** ME?!

WEAK!

AFTER 3 WEEKS JAZZY JAY HEADS BACK TO PLAYING CLUBS, MAKING MONEY, AND GETTING UNANIMOUS PRAISE. HOSTING DUTIES FALL INTO THE LAP OF THE NEXT **ZULU NATION** MEMBER IN LINE: **KOOL DJ RED ALERT.**

YEEEEEEAH!

KISS 987

HA!

HA HA! MARLEY, YOU'LL NEVER BELIEVE IT. THE NEW HOST ON THE KISS SHOW IS **KOOL DJ RED DIRT.**

KEEP TALKIN', **MAGIC.** YOU GONNA GET YOURS...

SINCE LEAVING HOME, **LAWRENCE PARKER** HAS CONSIDERED HIS LIFE IN THE STREETS AS A KIND OF **RELIGIOUS** JOURNEY.

SPENDING MUCH TIME IN THE **LIBRARY**, HE'S READ THAT ONE MUST COME NEAR DEATH TO GET CLOSE TO **GOD**.

YAWN...

HMMM...

HE DECIDES TO LET WHATEVER MAY HAPPEN TO HAPPEN. **LAISSEZ-FAIRE**... FOR THE MOST PART...

GOTTA BE $12 HERE...

I MUS' LOOK BUMMY...

A RAP CYPHER !!!

!

...AN' YOU LOOK **DOO-DOO** LIKE THAT BOY'S JEANS!!

HAW!

!!

HA HA HA HA HA HA!

PARKER HAS ACTUALLY BEEN PREPARING FOR A MOMENT LIKE THIS, AND HE HAS RHYMES IN THE CHAMBER TO PROVE IT. UNFORTUNATELY FOR YOU, DEAR READER, HIS FREESTYLE IS SO **HARDCORE**... SO **POWERFUL**... THAT THE WORDS CAN'T BE TRANSCRIBED WITHIN THESE PAGES. *

* THE **TRUTH** IS THAT WE DON'T KNOW THE EXACT RHYMES, AND WE WON'T FICTIONALIZE THE WORDS OF A **BLASTMASTER**.

THIS IS IT!

THIS IS IT!!

!!!

?

NEVER SAW NOTHIN'

FUNKY!

????

WOW

YOU KNOW 'IM?

WHO WUZZAT?

HUH?

?

NYC HAS ITS SHARE OF HOMELESS SHELTERS AND FOOD BANKS, WHICH LAWRENCE TAKES PLENTY ADVANTAGE OF. ONCE HE GETS HIS FILL, HE ENJOYS HELPING **HARE KRISHNAS** PASS OUT **VEGETARIAN** MEALS TO HIS BRETHREN.

PEACE, BROTHER...

HUH?

AS A GIFT, PARKER RECEIVES A FREE COPY OF THE BHAGAVAD GITA.

THERE HE BE!

KRISHNA !!!!

YO, THANKS FOR ALL 'AT GRUB EARLIER, **KRISHNA!**

HA HA!

HARE HARE...

...KRISHNA KRISHNA...

YOU GOTTA STOP CALLIN' ME THAT. MY NAME'S **LARRY.**

KRISHNA'S THE NAME OF THEIR **GOD**, YO!

IT WOULD BE LIKE CALLIN' ME...

...JESUS.

BUT YOU OUR GENIUS, KRISHNA!

HARE, HARE, KRISHNA, KRISHNA!

68

INTERESTINGLY ENOUGH, EVEN THOUGH **RAP** AND **HIP HOP** ARE GAINING MORE VISIBILITY IN THE STATES, THE **PREMIERE** OF THE FILM **WILD STYLE** MAKES ITS DEBUT IN **JAPAN** FIRST.

CHARLIE AHEARN, FAB FIVE FREDDY, AND EVERYBODY ELSE IN THE FLICK ARE BROUGHT TO THE LAND OF THE RISING SON TO TOUR WITH THE MOVIE FOR **THIRTY DAYS.**

Y'ALL DIG MY NEW DOME PIECE?

HAW!

HA HA HA **FRED!** HA HA HA

HA!

THE MERRY BLEND OF **BRONX** PIONEERS ARE HAPPY TO GIVE PERFORMANCES, DEMONSTRATIONS, AND ART TO THE PEOPLE OF **JAPAN.**

SAY "HO"!

凍しい

たわごと

GOOD TIMES ARE HAD BY ALL EVEN THOUGH SOME **BUGGIN' OUT** IS EXPECTED. **BUSY BEE STARSKI,** FOR EXAMPLE...

I'M THE AYATOLLAH...

...OF HIP HOP!

ONE DAY IN **YOYOGI PARK** THE **ROCKSTEADY CREW** HAPPENS UPON A GROUP OF **BOSOZOKU** GREASERS DANCING TO SOME VINTAGE AMERICAN **ROCK AND ROLL...**

ファンク

TOWARD THE END OF THE TOUR THE WILD STYLE CREW DOUBLES BACK TO SOME OF THE EARLIEST VENUES THEY VISITED.

FLASH? I THOUGHT YOU WAS ON THE TURN-TABLES?! WHO'S UP THERE? **DST**?

SOME JAPANESE KID. WHO'D HAVE THUNK?

SCOOBY DOO!!

ONCE THEY MAKE IT BACK TO THE STATES, THE FILM OPENS DOMESTICALLY AT THE **EMBASSY THEATER** ON **47TH** & **BROADWAY**. WITH HOMEFIELD ADVANTAGE THE SHOWINGS STEADILY SELL OUT WITH PEOPLE WATCHING IN AWE OF THEIR FRIENDS' FACES ON THE BIG SCREEN.

NG D!!

HA!

HEY, YO, BIZ GOTTA BIG-ASS HEAD AN' A SKINNY NECK!

HAW, LIKE A DUMDUM LOLLIPOP!

!!!

HAHA!

PSST!

SHHH!

Y'ALL STUPID!

BE QUIET ALREADY!

IT LOOK SO FAKE THOUGH...

HAW

IT IS FAKE IDIOT! 'SA DAMN MOVIE!

GOOFY

HO!

HE A SAY T

SHH!

THE SCREENINGS ARE SO STRONG, IN FACT, THAT **WILD STYLE** IS THE **#2** FILM IN **NEW YORK** THE WEEK THAT IT OPENS.

...TERMS OF ENDEARMENT, SHIT!

FUCK HOLLY-WOOD!

MC DJ FLAVOR

CHARLIE AHEARN THOUGHT THAT HE'D BE ABLE TO GET A MOMENTS REST NOW THAT THE FILM IS OUT OF HIS HANDS.

THESE KIDS ARE DESTROYIN' MY MOVIE HOUSE! THE WINDOWS GOT BUSTED... STOLE POSTERS!! EVERYTHING'S WROTE ON! YOU'RE GONNA HAVE TO PAY FOR ALL THIS!!

...I'm the director... HAVE YOU... EVER called SCORSESE at 3 A.M.?

RICK RUBIN IS BIG MAN ON NYU CAMPUS IN PART BECAUSE HIS FOLKS MADE SOME WILD PURCHASES ON HIS BEHALF. HIS DORM NEIGHBORS ARE PROBABLY THE FEW PEOPLE WHO AREN'T IMPRESSED.

RUBIN SPENDS LITTLE TIME IN CLASS AND SKATES BY HAVING HIS FILM GRAD STUDENT PAL RIC MENELLO GHOST WRITE HIS HOMEWORK.

MENELLO WILL GO ON TO STAR IN AND DIRECT SOME BEASTIE BOYS MUSIC VIDS.

LOTS OF RUBIN'S SCHEDULE IS TAKEN UP BY HIS BAND, HOSE. HONESTLY, LIKE MOST OF HIS EARLY INTERESTS, PLAYING MUSIC STARTS TO LACK ITS LUSTER.

HIT THE JUICE. THE WHITE NOISE WILL SOUND GREAT THROUGH THE MIC.

ONCE HE SITS BEHIND A MIXING BOARD AT POWER PLAY STUDIOS TO PRODUCE THE ACTUAL RECORD, RUBIN FEELS AT HOME.

SON, YOU CAN'T DO 'AT WITH THE KNOBS!!

WELL NOTHING IS BROKEN AND I LIKE THE WAY IT SOUNDS, MR. ENGINEER, SO IT STAYS, THANK YOU.

THE LOOK AND SOUND OF THE ENTIRE PACKAGE BECOMES RICK'S OBSESSION. HOSE'S 7-INCH RECORD IS NESTLED INSIDE A BROWN PAPER BAG.

DUDE, THAT IS HARDCORE!

PUNK AS FUCK!

NEW WAVE, EVEN.

THE "ARTCORE" SENSIBILITY OF THE GROUP IS VISUALLY CAPTURED IN THE GRAPHIC DESIGN OF THEIR 12-INCH RECORD WITH HOMAGE TO PIET MONDRIAN.

HOSE

EVERYTHING ABOUT THE RECORD IS LOVINGLY POLISHED BY RICK RUBIN, INCLUDING THIS STRIKING LOGO ON THE BACK OF THE SLEEVE.

Def Jam recordings

HANGING OUT WITH HIS AUNT, WHO WORKS AT ESTEE LAUDER, RICK HAS INSIDE ACCESS TO THE ART DEPARTMENT FACILITY, WHICH CONTAINS A SURPLUS OF ZIP-A-TONE SCREENS, PANTONE COLOR SWATCHES, AND LETRASET PRESS-ON TYPE.

WHEN DESIGNING THE **DEF JAM** LOGO, HIS IMPETUS FOR MAKING THE "D" AND "J" BIGGER THAN THE OTHER HELVETICA TYPOGRAPHY WAS TO HONOR THE **DJ**.

IF A COOL SONG IS A "**JAM**" THEN THE FRESHEST SONG WOULD BE A "**DEF JAM**."

I WONDER IF DEF IS "DEATH" OR DEF LIKE **DEFINITIVE**? I LIKE IT...

AFTER MOM AND DAD GOT THE RECORDS PRESSED, RICK RUBIN FEELS SOME RESPONSIBILITY TO TOUR HEAVILY AND PROMOTE THE VINYL. REALLY HE JUST WANTS TO MAKE SURE TO SELL ENOUGH RECORDS TO JUSTIFY MAKING **MORE** RECORDS.

MOBO!

MOBO!

HOSE ACTUALLY HAS RESPECT IN THE SCENE AND GETS TO PLAY WITH OTHER GROUPS LIKE **HUSKER DÜ**, **THE BUTTHOLE SURFERS**, **THE CIRCLE JERKS**, AND **REAGAN YOUTH**. LOCALLY IN **NYC** THE BAND WOULD SOMETIMES SHARE THE STAGE WITH THOSE BRATTY **BEASTIE BOYS**.

THE EGGS DID CRACK ON MOJO'S BACK!!!

IN THE TIME RUBIN HAS AVAILABLE HE ALSO HAS A RADIO SHOW ON **WYNU** THAT HE METICULOUSLY PROGRAMS.

I'VE GOT A NEW REKKID FOR YOU FROM THE **BEASTIES**. I WOULDN'T CALL IT **PUNK** AN' I'M NOT SURE IF IT'S **RAP**...

ON AIR

IT'S **COOKY-PUSS**. CHECK IT OUT!

TRY AS THEY MAY, THE **BEASTIE BOYS** CAN'T SEEM TO COME UP WITH ANY USABLE, FRESH MATERIAL FOR THEIR NEXT ALBUM. WHEN YOU BOOK A MUSIC STUDIO, TIME IS MONEY...

YO, B! RECORD THIS GOOD SHIT!

FOOLING AROUND WITH THE TIME THEY HAVE LEFT, A RANDOM PRANK PHONECALL TO THE **CARVEL ICE CREAM** 800 NUMBER IS IN ORDER. NATURALLY, THEY RECORD THE EXCHANGE.

WHERE YO' SOOPA VIZA AT?

I GOT THE NUMBER ANYWAY, BABY!

MICHAEL DIAMOND DOING HIS BEST KINGFISH IMPERSONATION

...OR DID ADAM HOROVITZ DO THIS PART?

THAT BITCH HANG UP ON ME?

HAHA, YOU KNOW WE COULD PUT A **RAP** BEAT UNDERNEATH THIS. SCRATCH SOME RECORDS...

I BET THE DOWNTOWN ART DORKS WILL THINK IT'S AS COOL AS **BUFFALO GALS**.

...AND THAT'S BASICALLY WHAT THEY DO. AFTER CUTTING SOME **STEVE MARTIN** RECORDS INTO THE MIX THEY BUST OUT A FEW MORE SONGS FOR FLAVOR AND THE **COOKY PUSS** ALBUM IS BORN.

FIGURES **THIS** WOULD BE THE MOST **POPULAR** SONG OF OURS.

HOW THE HECK CAN WE PLAY THIS LIVE AT SHOWS?

WE JUST GOTTA GET US A **DJ**.

TOM CARVEL IS NONE-TOO-HAPPY WITH WHAT HE PERCEIVES AS A MOCKERY. HE'D **SUE** IF HIS NEPHEW WASN'T SUCH A BIG FAN OF THE RECORD.

COOKIE PUSS

© CARVEL

DIGGING DEEP ENOUGH YOU CAN FIND SOME GREAT VIDEO CLIPS OF THE BEASTIE BOYS FROM THIS PERIOD WHEN THEY WERE ON THE **SCOTT AND GARY CABLE ACCESS SHOW.**

NOBODY LIKES TO PAY US ANYTHING.

WE'RE STILL OWED LIKE $6000 FOR THE COOKY PUSS DEAL...

HYPING UP THEIR REVIEW IN THE BRITISH MAGAZINE THE FACE

A MOCK **REGGAE** SONG ON THE COOKY PUSS RECORD CALLED **BEASTIE REVOLUTION** SOMEHOW ENDS UP BEING **SAMPLED** IN A **BRITISH AIRWAYS** COMMERCIAL WITHOUT PERMISSION.

THE TEENAGERS POOL THEIR RESOURCES TO SUE THE AIRLINE AND THEY END UP WITH $40,000 OUT OF THE DEAL.

WE GOT MONEY LIKE **CHARLES DICKENS!**

THIS IS HOW THEY'RE ABLE TO AFFORD THEIR FIRST APARTMENT AT **59 CHRYSTIE ST.**

WHO THE FUCK COVERS THE FLOOR OF THEIR CRIB WITH ASPHALT?

IT WAS DEFINITELY A SELLING POINT.

IF ONE IS TO BELIEVE IN THE "10,000 HOURS RULE OF MASTERY," THIS IS WHERE THE BEASTIES ACCUMULATED A SUBSTANTIAL AMOUNT OF THAT PRACTICE.

BANG!

HUH?

OH YEAH, THERE'S ALL SORTS OF DRAMA THAT TAKES PLACE AT THE **SWEATSHOP** ABOVE THEIR APARTMENT...

THEY SHOT THROUGH THE FRICKIN' CEILING!!

MAN, THIS IS MY MOM'S TOASTER OVEN!

...BUT THE "TENANTS" ALWAYS CLEAN UP THEIR MESSES WITHOUT MAKING A SCENE.

NO, NUH T'ING IS WONG.

SANK YOU.

YOU'RE AXING ME ABOUT MY REKKID *BEAT BOP*? YOU WANNA KNOW ABOUT *BASQUIAT*?

JEAN-MICHEL BASQUIAT IS A PUPPET OF THE *LIGHT DWELLERS*... HE'S A *CULTURE-VULTURE* AND HE BARELY HAD *ANYTHING* TO DO WITH MY REKKID...

"*FAB FIVE FREDDY* PUT ME, THE *RAMMELLZEE*, ON A MISSION TO INTERROGATE BASQUIAT... TO FEEL HIM OUT. HOMEBOY WAS GETTING BIG NUTS AN' WE NEEDED TO SEE WHOSE SIDE HE WAS ON IN OUR *ICONOKLASTIK WARFARE.*"

...I CAN DO THIS SHIT CHEW DO, NO PROBLEM, BUT YOU AIN'T IN MY LEAGUE. YOU CAN'T PAINT *BURNERS*...

...YOU GOT *ZERO* RHYMES!

HA HA HA! WE SHALL SEE...

"...WOULDN'T YOU KNOW THIS FOOL PUT ME TO THE TEST THE VERY NEXT DAY."

...AN' YA DON'T STOP !!!

STAGE ONE IS COMPLETE. NOW I'LL SET THE PRICE AN' SEE IF YOUR CANVASES COLLECT DUST.

" OF COURSE MY PAINTINGS SOLD OUT OF THE *ANNINA NOSEI GALLERY* IN PICO-SECONDS. IT SOON BECAME TIME TO SEE HOW THIS *CRUMB-CRUSHER* STACKED UP IN OUR HIP HOP UNIVERSE."

YOU KNOW YOUR SKILLS IS WEAK, RIGHT?

...EVER THINK ABOUT MAKING A *RECORD* ?

YEAH...

"BASQUIAT FLIPPED THE SCRIP' ON ME AN' BEFORE I KNEW IT I WAS IN THIS *RECORDING FORTRESS* WIF A 15-YEAR OLD *K-ROB*. JEAN-MICHEL HAD THE NERVE TO TRY AN' MAKE US USE HIS LYRICS."

YOU A ARTIST! *WE* THE EMCEES!

I'LL PLAY A *PIMP* ON THE STREET CORNER. *ROB*, YOU BE A SCHOOL KID WALKIN' HOME...

"OF COURSE WE WAS HARD AS HELL, BUT **BEAT-BOP** WAS JUST A TEST RECORDING FAR AS I'M CONCERNED. BASQUIAT'S **ONLY** CONTRIBUTION TO THE PACKAGE WAS TO FRONT THE EN'S TO PRESS THE REKKID!"

DEF DEF DEF JAM Y'ALL! I'M LIKE A B-BOY MAKIN' WIT' THE FREAK FREAK!

MAYBE RICK RUBIN HEARD THIS WHEN DECIDING ON A NAME FOR HIS LABEL?

"I GUESS HE DID DO THE **ARTWORK** FOR THE SLEEVE AN' SHIT... EVEN THEN HE COLD-**DISSED** ME SPELLING **RAMMELLZEE** WITH ONE 'L'! MY NAME IS A BALANCED BATTLE OF CULTURE! **TWO 'L'S!!!**"

FIGURED WE'D START OFF WITH 500.

TO DATE, THE ORIGINAL PRESSING OF BEAT BOP IS PROBABLY THE MOST VALUABLE HIP HOP RECORD.

IT'S ALSO PROBABLY THE CHEAPEST BASQUIAT ART PRINT YOU CAN BUY.

"I THINK THAT SAME YEAR 'JOHN-MICHELLE' SOLD OUR **BOOTLEG-ASS** SONG TO **PROFILE REKKIDS**. YOU KNOW WHAT THEM MUH-FUCKAZ SAID WHEN I WENT UP TO THEY OFFICE TO GET SOME **MO' MONEY**?"

SON, YOU ALREADY MAKE ENOUGH MONEY...

"IN FACK, WHEN **BASQUIAT'S** DUMB-ASS SHOT HIMSELF TO **DEF** WITH HAIR-ON, THE **FOO'** DIDN'T EVEN CASH THE PROFILE REKKIDS CHECK, I FOUND OUT."

"PEOPLE SAY **BEAT BOP** WAS ARTSY... EXPERIMENTAL... **INFLUENTIAL**! THEY SAY IT WAS AN ACHIEVEMENT. CATS TELL ME THAT MY VOICE AND DELIVERY WAS **GROUNDBREAKING**. IT'S ALL AN UNFINISHED MESS. I WAS JUST USING THE VOICE OF MY CHARACTER, BARSHAW GANGSTARR - THE **DRAGON DUCK**!"

CYPRESS HILL

AMONG OTHER THINGS I GUESS YOU CAN SAY THAT **RAMMELLZEE** WAS AN INSPIRATION ON MY STYLE...

HAD TO THINK OF SOMETHING. **MUGGS** AND **SEN DOG** HATED MY NORMAL DELIVERY.

BEASTIE BOYS

PUTTIN' SONGS TOGETHER AIN'T NO PUZZLE LIKE **YAHTZEE**, SENDIN' THIS ONE OUT TO **K-ROB** AND **RAMMELLZEE**!

WELL, LET ME INTRO-DUCE MYSELF ON THIS **CUT**. I'M **ADROCK**, I'M LIT LIKE A **MOTHER-FUCK**!

KEITH LEBLANC, THE SESSION-PLAYING DRUMMER FOR SUGAR HILL, HAS FOUND INSPIRATION IN READING THE AUTOBIOGRAPHY OF MALCOLM X AS TOLD TO ALEX HALEY.

HEY, SUGAR HILL OWNS ALL THOSE OLD CHESS RECORDS RECORDINGS OF MALCOLM X, NO?

SO WHAT?

DOUG WIMBISH

MARSHALL CHESS IS ACCESSIBLE TO LEBLANC BECAUSE HE'S HELPING SUGAR HILL WITH THE INVENTORY OF HIS FATHER'S RECORD COMPANY.

SO YOU USED ONE OF THESE NEW DRUM MACHINES TO CREATE A HIP HOP BEAT UNDERNEATH CAREFULLY CHOSEN PHRASES FROM MALCOLM X?

THIS IS GENIUS, MAN. BETTY SHABAZZ NEEDS TO HEAR THIS!

NO SELL OUT!

YA THINK?

MALCOLM X'S WIDOW BETTY ISN'T HARD TO FIND WORKING IN THE ADMINISTRATION OFFICE AT MEDGAR EVERS COLLEGE.

MS. SHABAZZ, I... UH... UMM... HAVE...

NO NEED FOR PREAMBLES, SON.

THE RECORD WILL SPEAK FOR ITSELF...

...I'LL EITHER LIKE IT OR I WON'T!

DAYS LATER KEITH GETS A CALL FROM BETTY.

KEITH, YOU ARE A VERY TALENTED MUSICIAN, THANK YOU...

BUT CAN YOU PLEASE NOT END THE SONG WITH A DAMNED GUNSHOT?

WITH MS. SHABAZZ'S APPROVAL, KEITH GETS THE GUMPTION TO SEE IF SYLVIA ROBINSON WOULD LIKE TO PUBLISH THE RECORD.

I'LL GET BACK TO YOU WITH SOME CHANGES...

UH...

WEEKS GO BY WITHOUT WORD FROM SUGAR HILL. IT'S A BREEZE FOR KEITH TO FIND A HOME FOR THE RECORD ELSEWHERE.

MR. MAGIC'S RAP ATTACK WITH A NEW RECORD FROM **TOMMY BOY!**

MALCOLM X! NO SELL OUT!!

THIS, OF COURSE, DOESN'T ESCAPE THE EARS OF **SYLVIA ROBINSON.**

REMEMBER THE RECORD OUR WHITE BOY MADE A WHILE BACK?

I WANT A FEW **THOUSAND** PRESSED UP AT A HELLUVA PACE!

IN TURN, KEITH LEBLANC AND **TOMMY BOY** RECORDS DISCOVER THE SAME SONG RELEASED AS **MALCOLM X NO SELL OUT** BY THE **SUGAR-HILL ALL STARS.**

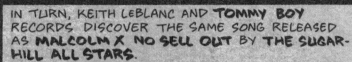

OBJECTION!

THE FIRST TIME SYLVIA MEETS **BETTY SHABAZZ** IN COURT...

MS. SHABAZZ, MA'AM, IT'S SO NICE TO...

KEEP ON MOVING, YOU PIRATE!!

THINGS APPEAR TO GO DOWNHILL FOR SUGAR HILL FROM HERE...

EXCUSE ME. WHERE IS MS. **GANGSTER**?

I MEAN, MS. **ROBINSON**...

THE SETTLEMENT DETERMINES THAT **TOMMY BOY** HAS THE RIGHTS TO RELEASE THE RECORD AND **SUGAR HILL** WILL GET A BACK-END ROYALTY ON EACH COPY SOLD.

EVEN STILL WE BES' BE CAREFUL...

WE AIN'T BRINGIN' IN ENOUGH EN'S TO KEEP FIGHTIN' COURT CASES...

THE SONG DISAPPEARS FROM THE AIRWAVES. IT'S SPECU-LATED THAT SUGAR HILL HAS SOMETHING TO DO WITH IT.

ON SECOND THOUGHT IT MIGHT NOT BE COOL PUTTING THE MAN'S WORDS OVER TOP DANCE MUSIC.

BECAUSE OF THE TREMENDOUS LEGAL FEES, TOMMY BOY HAS NO ROYALTIES TO TRICKLE DOWN TO BETTY AND KEITH.

HOW THE **HELL** DO YOU GET PAID IN THIS RECORD BUSINESS?

REGARDLESS OF ALL THE DRAMA, THE RECORD IS AN INSTANT CLASSIC AND IS HEARD BY ALL THE **RIGHT** PEOPLE...

NOW **THIS** IS ON THE RIGHT TRACK.

MC CHUCKY D

STRONG ISLAND REPRESENT

...SO I AXED THIS GIRL FOR A **DIME**. THE GIRL WAS **FINE**. SHE WAS SO **DIVINE**...

...THEN I CALLED THE OJ FROM THE **PHONE**, UP PULLED A CAR WITH A LIGHT GREEN **TONE**...

...I GOT IN THE CAR, SO DID THE **FREAK**, WE GOT SO HIGH AND SHE KISSED MY **CHEEK**...

... WENT TO HER HOUSE, I PAID AND GOT **OUT**, WHAT HAPPENED THAT NIGHT Y'ALL KNOW **ABOUT**...

THEE! IT'TH TOO HAWD!

RUSS, YOU'RE AN **IDIOT**! DARRYL'S THE BEST RAPPER OUT THERE!

SOMEHOW, DESPITE **RUSSELL SIMMONS'** TREPIDATION, **RUN** AND **D** ARE ABLE TO WEASEL THEIR WAY INTO **LARRY SMITH'S** ATTIC STUDIO.

IF Y'ALL WAYTHT MY TIME I'LL KILL Y'ALL BOF TO **DEF**!

LARRY, WE NEED THE BEAT STRIPPED DOWN. NO **SUGAR HILL** FOO-FOO SOUNDIN' GARBAGE!

NO INSTRUMENTS!

GOTCHA.

RUSSELL "RUSH" COMBS THROUGH DARRYL'S RHYME NOTEBOOK FOR ALL THE BEST SELECTIONS.

... AND AFTER I SAY " **IT'S LIKE THAT**.."

"YOU SAY "**AN' THAT'S THE WAY IT IS**..."

BET!

THEY CONSCIOUSLY PATTERN THEIR DELIVERY TO PLAY OFF EACH OTHER LIKE THE BEST ROUTINES FROM THE **COLD CRUSH BROTHERS** ROUTINES.

MONEY IS THE KEY TO END ALL YOUR **WOES**...

...YOUR UPS, YOUR DOWNS, YOUR HIGHS, AND YOUR **LOWS**...

IT'S LIKE THAT CREATES A POWERFUL ENERGY IN THE ROOM.

THINKIN' ABOUT IT I HAVE A BEAT THAT'S EVEN MORE STRIPPED DOWN THAN THIS...

LARRY HAD PROGRAMMED A DRUM MACHINE TO MIMIC THE PERCUSSION FROM HIS BAND ORANGE KRUSH'S SONG ACTION.

WHAT IF WE PUT JUTH'T A LITTLE MELODY TO THE TRACK?

HELL NAW!

NO CORNY STUFF, RUSSELL-MAN!

THE BOYS CONVINCE THE RECORD VETERANS THAT VOCALS AND LYRICS WILL BE THE SELLING POINT.

TWO YEARS AGO, A FRIEND OF MINE AXED ME TO SAY SOME EMCEE RHYMES...

... SO I SAID THE WORDS I'M ABOUT TO SAY... THE RHYMES WERE DEF AND IT WENT THIS WAY...

I'M DMC, IN THE PLACE TO BE, I WENT TO SAINT JOHN'S UNIVERSITY...

...SINCE KINNY-GARDEN I ACQUIRED THE KNOWLEDGE AND AFTER 12TH GRADE I WENT STRAIGHT TO COLLEGE...

I HAD NO FUCKING CLUE Y'ALL COULD RHYME LIKE THITH...

WE GOT A REKKID HERE!

WE GOT A REKKID WE CAN THELL!!

DOUGLAS DIFRANCO AND **STEVE STEIN** ARE IN THE OFFICE OF **TOMMY BOY RECORDS** TO PICK UP THEIR AWARD, WHICH INCLUDES $100, THE COMPANY'S BACK CATALOG, A FEW T-SHIRTS, AND A PROMISE TO HAVE THEIR MIX PRESSED AND DISTRIBUTED TO CLUBS AND RADIO STATIONS. TOMMY BOY CEO **TOM SILVERMAN** LAMENTS...

IT WOULD BE JUST MY LUCK! OUT OF **70+** ENTRIES TO MY CONTEST...

...THE WINNERS, HANDS DOWN, WOULD BE TWO UNMARKETABLE OLD **WHITE** GUYS, HA HA HA...

ha ha... THANKS.

STEVE STEIN, THE **32-YEAR-OLD** AD-FIRM COPY-WRITER, REMEMBERS HIS INTRODUCTION TO **HIP HOP**. IT HAPPENED WHEN HE INADVERTENTLY TAPED A RADIO SHOW THAT HAD **CHRIS STEIN** AND **DEBBIE HARRY** FROM **BLONDIE** AS GUEST DJ'S.

SEARCHIN' FOR THE PERFECT BEAT...

LIVE AT THE **ROXY** EVERY FRIDAY? I'M SO THERE!

HIS FIRST NIGHT OUT HE'S **HOOKED** BY **AFRIKA BAMBAATAA'S** ECLECTIC MIXOLOGY.

3-6-9, THE GOOSE DRANK **WINE**, THE MONKEY CHEW TO-BACCO ON THE STREET CAR **LINE**...

THE LINE **BROKE**, THE MONKEY GOT **CHOKED**, AND THEY ALL WENT TO HEAVEN IN A LITTLE ROW **BOAT**...

AS A SUCCESSFUL GUY IN THE **ADVERTISING** WORLD, **STEIN** HAS THE EXTRANEOUS INCOME TO BUY ALL THE FUNKY RECORDS HE HEARS IN THE CLUBS.

YOU COULDN'T UNDERSTAND THE VIRTUE OF THIS RECORD UNTIL YOU SEE PEOPLE SPINNING ON THEIR HEADS WHILE LISTENING.

BY DAY, STEIN WORKS WITH **DOUGLAS DIFRANCO**, STUDIO ENGINEER MASTER, TO COBBLE TOGETHER RADIO COMMERCIALS PACKED WITH INFORMATION.

BY NIGHT, THE DUO SEEKS OUT ANY GOOD HIP HOP PARTIES THEY CAN FIND...

MARY, MARY...

...WHERE YA GOIN' TO?

TOMMY BOY PUBLISHED A SONG BY **G.L.O.B.E** & **WHIZ KID** CALLED **PLAY THAT BEAT MR. D.J.** IT'S A WELL-PRODUCED RECORD, BUT THE COMPANY NEEDS TO CULTIVATE MORE INTEREST.

PLAY IT ON THE PLAY-GROUND...

PLAY IT IN THE STREET!

A RECORD REMIX CONTEST IS DEVISED AND SOLICITED IN **BILLBOARD MAGAZINE** THAT MONTH. A MUTUAL FRIEND KNOWS THAT STEIN AND DIFRANCO ARE HIP HOP FANS AND HE MAKES THEM AWARE...

THIS COULD BE FUN.

CAN'T GO WRONG IF WE TREAT IT LIKE JUST ANOTHER COMMERCIAL GIG.

STEVE STEIN'S MAJOR CONTRIBUTION TO THE PROJECT IS HIS EXPANSIVE RECORD COLLECTION, HIS INSIGHT, AND HIS SUGGESTIONS, WHICH RANGE FROM **LITTLE RICHARD** TO **PEECH BOYS** TO **HUMPHREY BOGART** AND BEYOND.

WHAT DO YOU THINK ABOUT THIS **CULTURE CLUB** PIECE?

DIFRANCO IS THE TECHNICAL GENIUS AND LORD OF THE RECORDING EQUIPMENT. IT'S HIS JOB TO ALSO KEEP THE BEAT AMONGST THE CHAOS AND TO MAKE IT ALL WORK.

NO PROB.

KEEP 'EM COMING!

THE ADVERTISING BIZ IS A PRETTY SQUARE, MONDAY-FRIDAY, 9-5 ENTERPRISE, SO THEY HAVE THE WEEKEND TO CREATE THE **PAYOFF MIX**, WHICH TROUNCES THE COMPETITION UNANIMOUSLY. **STEVE STEIN** AND **DOUGLAS DIFRANCO** ARE VERY CONSCIOUS OF THEIR NAMES WHEN SUBMITTING...

AIN'T NO SURPRISE... THE WINNER IS...

AFRIKA BAMBAATAA

ARTHUR BAKER

DOUBLE DEE AND STEINSKI. THE PAYOFF MIX.

JELLY BEAN BENITEZ

THE PAYOFF MIX IS AN IMMEDIATE SENSATION AND IS OFT-REQUESTED WHEREVER IT'S HEARD. UNFORTUNATELY BECAUSE IT'S IMPOSSIBLE TO CLEAR ALL THE SAMPLES THE MIX CAN'T BE LEGALLY RELEASED.

YOU THINK IT'S CRAZY THAT BOOTLEGS GO FOR $20 A TAPE HERE?

THEY GO FOR $60 IN EUROPE.

DOUBLE DEE & **STEINSKI** ARE HAPPY TO HAVE AN UNDERGROUND SMASH HIT, BUT THE **EXTRALEGAL** EFFORT WON'T PAY THE BILLS.

WORD FROM MADISON AVENUE...

...APPLE COMPUTER HAS A SUPER BOWL SPOT IN THE WORKS THAT'S SUPPOSED TO BE GREAT.

IN **1983** JOURNEYMAN EMCEE **SPOONIE GEE** SNEAKS AWAY FROM **SUGAR HILL** TO CREATE A GROUP CALLED THE **BOO DAH BLISS CREW**. HE GOES UNNAMED TO AVOID **LEGAL** ENTANGLEMENTS ON THEIR ONE AND ONLY RECORD, **PASS THE BOO DAH**. THE WHOLE ENTERPRISE IS REALLY JUST A VEHICLE TO SHOWCASE SPOONIE'S FRIEND AND NEIGHBOR, **DOUG E. FRESH**.

CLICK CLICK CLICK GULP

AFTER THE DIVESTITURE OF **FLASH & THE FURIOUS**, **MELLE MEL** BECOMES THE CROWN PRINCE OF THE **SUGAR HILL** LABEL, AND THEY FIGURE IT'S TIME HE RELEASED A **NEW** RECORD.

CAN'T WE JUS' CALL IT "**MELLE MEL**" OR "**GRANDMASTER MELLE MEL**"? PEOPLE COULD CONFUSE IT FOR ANOTHER **FLASH** RECORD!

AND YOUR POINT IS?

THE NEW SONG BY "**GRANDMASTER & MELLE MEL**" IS CALLED **WHITE LINES**, AND IT STARTED AS A PARTY RECORD INSPIRED BY **DJ JUNEBUG**, BUT AFTER HIS **DEATH** IT'S TAKEN A MORE **OMINOUS** TONE.

ATHLETES **REJECTED** GOVERNORS **CORRECTED** GANGSTERS, THUGS AND SMUGGLERS ARE THOROUGHLY **RESPECTED**. THE MONEY GETS **DIVIDED**...

THE WOMEN GET **EXCITED**. NOW I'M BROKE AND IT'S NO JOKE... IT'S HARD AS HELL TO **FIGHT IT, DON'T BUY IT! UGH!**

SUGAR HILL IS NOTORIOUSLY CHEAP, SO WHEN **SPIKE LEE**, A YOUNG **NYU** FILM STUDENT, OFFERS TO SHOOT A MUSIC VIDEO FOR THE SONG, HE'S DENIED A BUDGET. USING HIS OWN RESOURCES, SPIKE CASTS A 22-YEAR-OLD **LAURENCE FISHBURNE** IN THE MAIN ROLE AS A SPECTRAL **DRUG DEALER**.

TURNS OUT THAT THE **SUGAR HILL HOUSE BAND** CO-OPTED THE **BASSLINE** FROM A NEW, UNDER-GROUND TUNE CALLED **CAVERN** BY THE BAND **LIQUID LIQUID.** SOME LYRICS WERE ALSO "BORROWED."

"SLIP IN AND OUT OF PHENOMENON"

"SLIP IN AND OUT OF PHENOMENON"

WHITE LINES IS RELEASED AT THE RIGHT PLACE, RIGHT TIME... AND MAKES THE **BILLBOARD** CHARTS. **ED BAHLMAN,** THE **OWNER** OF LIQUID LIQUID'S LABEL, **99 RECORDS,** ALMOST IMMEDIATELY FILES SUIT.

ARE YOU **CRAZY!**

WHY THE **HELL** WOULD I "GO FOR A RIDE" WITH YOU SUGAR HILL **GANGSTERS**?

THE 99 RECORDS LABEL IS RUN OUT OF A STORE BY THE SAME NAME ON 99 MACDOUGAL STREET IN GREENWICH VILLAGE. IT COULD ALL BE TOTALLY UNRELATED, **BUT** THE AMOUNT OF VANDALISM AND THEFT RISES TO ASTRONOMICAL LEVELS WHEN THE ISSUE IS BROUGHT TO COURT.

THE CASE GRUELINGLY DRAGS ON TO A VERY **EXPENSIVE** DEGREE UNTIL THE COURT FINALLY RULES IN FAVOR OF **99 RECORDS.** AS PART OF THE SETTLEMENT THEY ARE DUE $600,000, BUT...

SUGAR HILL WILL BE FILING FOR **BANK-RUPTCY,** NOW.

SORRY!

RUINED BY THE LEGAL BILLS, ED BAHLMAN SHUTTERS HIS BUSINESS AND THE MEMBERS OF LIQUID LIQUID DISBAND.

SNAP!

IN 1995 WHEN *DURAN DURAN* COVERED *WHITE LINES,* LIQUID LIQUID DECIDED TO BRING THE ISSUE UP IN COURT AND FINALLY CAME AWAY SATISFIED WITH AN UNDISCLOSED SETTLEMENT, MORE THAN A *DECADE* AFTER MAKING *CAVERN.*

SOMETHIN' LIKE A PHENOMENON...

SOMETHIN' LIKE A PHENOMENON...

AFTER **RUN** AND **D** FINISHED THEIR DEMO, **RUSSELL** "**RUSH**" SET TO WORK KNOCKING ON THE DOORS OF EVERY **MAJOR** RECORD COMPANY IN AMERICA...

BLACK EXECUTIVES WERE ESPECIALLY NOT IM-PRESSED...

PROFILE RECORDS, HOME OF DR. JECKYLL & MR. HYDE, FINDS THE DEMO TO BE ADEQUATE FOR THEIR "SINGLE-A-MONTH" BUSINESS MODEL.

GIVE LITH $4,000!

WE'RE THINKIN' $2,000. TAKE IT OR LEAVE IT.

THOLD!

WHAT ARE THEIR NAMES NOW? RUN AND D THE MC? I DON'T LIKE IT. HOW ABOUT RUN-DMC?

NO PROB.

...AND THE B-SIDE... KRUSH GROOVE? THEY SAY "SUCKER MC'S" A LOT. WE'LL USE THAT AS THE TITLE.

YOU'RE THE BAWTH.

THE SUSTAINABLE SUCCESS OF PROFILE IS PARTIALLY DUE TO THEIR KNOWLEDGE OF THE KEY CLUB DJ'S TO SUPPLY RECORDS, WHO THEN REPORT POPULARITY TO RADIO STATIONS.

HERE'S ANOTHER POINT IN LIFE YOU SHOULD NOT MISS!

DO NOT BE A FOOL WHO'S PREJUDICE...

ONCE BROADCAST, IT DOESN'T TAKE LONG FOR RUN-DMC'S RECORD IT'S LIKE THAT/SUCKER MC'S TO BEGIN SELLING 20,000 COPIES A WEEK.

WAY IT IS!

LAGUARDIA COMMUNITY COLLEGE...

THIS IS MY REKKID!!!!

HUH!

DMC TAKES A LEAVE OF ABSENCE FROM ST. JOHN'S UNIVERSITY...

RUSSELL WAS RIGHT EVERY STEP OF THE WAY!

SHOULDN'T AH DOUBTED 'IM.

JASON MIZELL

THE ICONOCLASTIC **HERBIE HANCOCK** HAS ALREADY BROUGHT FUNK, SYNTHESIZERS, AND A CERTAIN WHIMSY TO THE **JAZZ** WORLD, AND ON HIS NEXT ALBUM PROJECT, **FUTURE SHOCK**, HE'S ENLISTED PRODUCER **BILL LASWELL** TO LEAVE NO STONE UNTURNED IN THE SPIRIT OF FINDING UNUSUAL SOUNDS...

BAM, I WANT A **SCRATCH DJ** TO PLAY ON MY RECORD. WHO'S THE **BEST**?

WHIZ KID IS DOPE...

...BUT **DST** CAN SHINE, TOO.

WHO?

GRAND MIXER DST. YOU CAN'T MISS 'EM.

ARMED WITH ELECTRONICS—COMPUTERS, KEYBOARDS, TURNTABLES—AND A STRATEGIC COPY OF **FAB FIVE FREDDY'S CHANGE THE BEAT**, LASWELL, DST, AND THE BAND **MATERIAL** SET TO WORK IN A BROOKLYN RECORDING STUDIO ON A SONG CALLED **ROCKIT**.

FRESH...

LASWELL DIGS THE FREEDOM OF THIS EXPERIMENTAL RECORD AND DEVISES A WAY TO TEST IT ON A CROWD ONE DAY WHILE SHOPPING FOR SPEAKERS.

NO, I DON'T LISTEN TO THAT SHIT.

LET ME HEAR HOW THIS TAPE SOUNDS WITH THESE SPEAKERS.

YES, SIR.

WOW!

NOW SIR, I MUST WARN YOU THAT THE FIDELITY OF VINYL IS FAR SUPERIOR TO YOUR TAPE.

I GOTTA **COP** IT!!

THIS THE JAM!

IT'S AIGHT, I GUESS...

BUGGED OUT!!

WHAT IS DIS?

WHO?

AIDED BY AN UNFORGETTABLE AWARD-WINNING MUSIC VIDEO, **ROCKIT** CLIMBS THE CHARTS FASTER THAN ANYONE CAN IMAGINE.

THE MORE **IMPORTANT** TELEVISION BROADCAST IS THE LIVE ROCKIT PERFORMANCE BY **HERBIE HANCOCK** AND CO. AT THE **1984 GRAMMYS**, WHERE THEY ALSO **WIN** THE AWARD FOR "BEST R&B INSTRUMENTAL."

THE REASON THE BROADCAST IS CRUCIAL IS BECAUSE, AT THE SAME TIME, ALL ACROSS THE COUNTRY, **FUTURE DJ'S** ARE DISCOVERING HOW GRANDMIXER DST GOT THOSE WEIRD NOISES...

MIXMASTER MIKE 14 YEARS OLD	**ROC RAIDA** 12 YEARS OLD	**DJ QBERT** 15 YEARS OLD	**ROB SWIFT** 12 YEARS OLD

WITH A SPARE **$250** BURNING A HOLE IN HIS POCKET, **ADAM HOROVITZ** HAD EVERY INTENTION OF BUYING A **PAUL WELLER RICKENBACKER GUITAR**.

...I SAID "**FUCK IT**," I ALREADY GOT A GUITAR.

WHY WE NEED A **DRUM MACHINE**? **KATE** CAN PLAY DRUMS. **I** CAN PLAY DRUMS...

OH YEAH! I BUMPED INTO **DAVE SKILKEN**. THERE'S A PARTY AT **NYU** CAMPUS TONIGHT.

THERE'S A **PARTY** AT NYU CAMPUS **EVERY** NIGHT!

5 UNIVERSITY PLACE...

TRUST ME...

...THIS PARTY WILL BE MORE **LIVE**!

FUCK, I ALWAYS FORGET WHICH IS **HIS**.

ROOM 712...

HERE IT IS!

HUH...

BUBBLES!

RICK RUBIN!

BEASTIES!

HEY, I JUST CAME FROM OFF TOUR AN' GOT THE **DEFFEST** RAP REKKID.

SUCKER MC'S!?

IT'S CALLED... UH...

SUCKER MC'S OR SOMESUCH...

IT'S **FINALLY** BEEN DONE! A **RAP REKKID** THAT HAS THE SAME **ENERGY** AS THE LIVE **SHIT**!

THIS **AIN'T** SOME NOVELTY **DISCO** KNOCK OFF! IT'S **REAL** HIP HOP ON **WAX**!

I CAN MAKE A **BETTER** ONE, THOUGH.

I'M GONNA MAKE A **RAP REKKID**.

KNOW **ANYONE** WITH A **DRUM MACHINE**?

RUN-DMC IS ALREADY A **HIT** ON THE **RADIO** AND ON **WAX** BY THE TIME **RUSSELL** BOOKS THEIR FIRST LIVE PERFORMANCE TOGETHER AT AN **AFTER-SCHOOL** FUNCTION IN **NEW JERSEY**.

YOU SHOULD HAVE GONE TO SCHOOL!

YOU COULD HAVE LEARNED A TRADE!

PARENTS WELCOME

THE DUO IS MORE EXCITED FOR THE GIG THEY'RE ALSO BOOKED TO PLAY THAT SAME NIGHT. IF NOT FOR **RUSSELL SIMMONS**, AN UNTESTED CREW WOULD **NEVER** GET TO START OUT PLAYING HERE, POPULAR RECORD OR NOT.

HOME OF

TIS LOW · GRANDMASTER FLASH · DR. JECKYLL & MR. HYDE · SEQUENCE · SPO GEE

DISCO FEVER

"SWEET G" · LOVEBUG STARSKI · JUNEBUG · COLD CRUSH BROS.

ONCE THE **FEVER BELIEVERS** HAVE A FEW FACES TO PUT WITH THE SONGS.

THESE BOYS SELL CARS OR SUMPIN'? HUH?

LOOKIT DIS!!

HA HA

HAW!!

GO BACK TO QUEENS WIT' THIS SHIT!!

BUT IS THEY **SERIOUS** AT ALL?

A DEBRIEFING SESSION AFTER THE TRIAL BY FIRE...

Y'ALL WILL GET THE TH'TAGE TH'TUFF DOWN WITH REPITITION...

...BUT, THUMP-THING ELTH ITH MITHING.

JASON "JAZZY JASE" MIZELL

WHY YOU LOOKIN' AT ME LIKE THAT, RUSSELL?

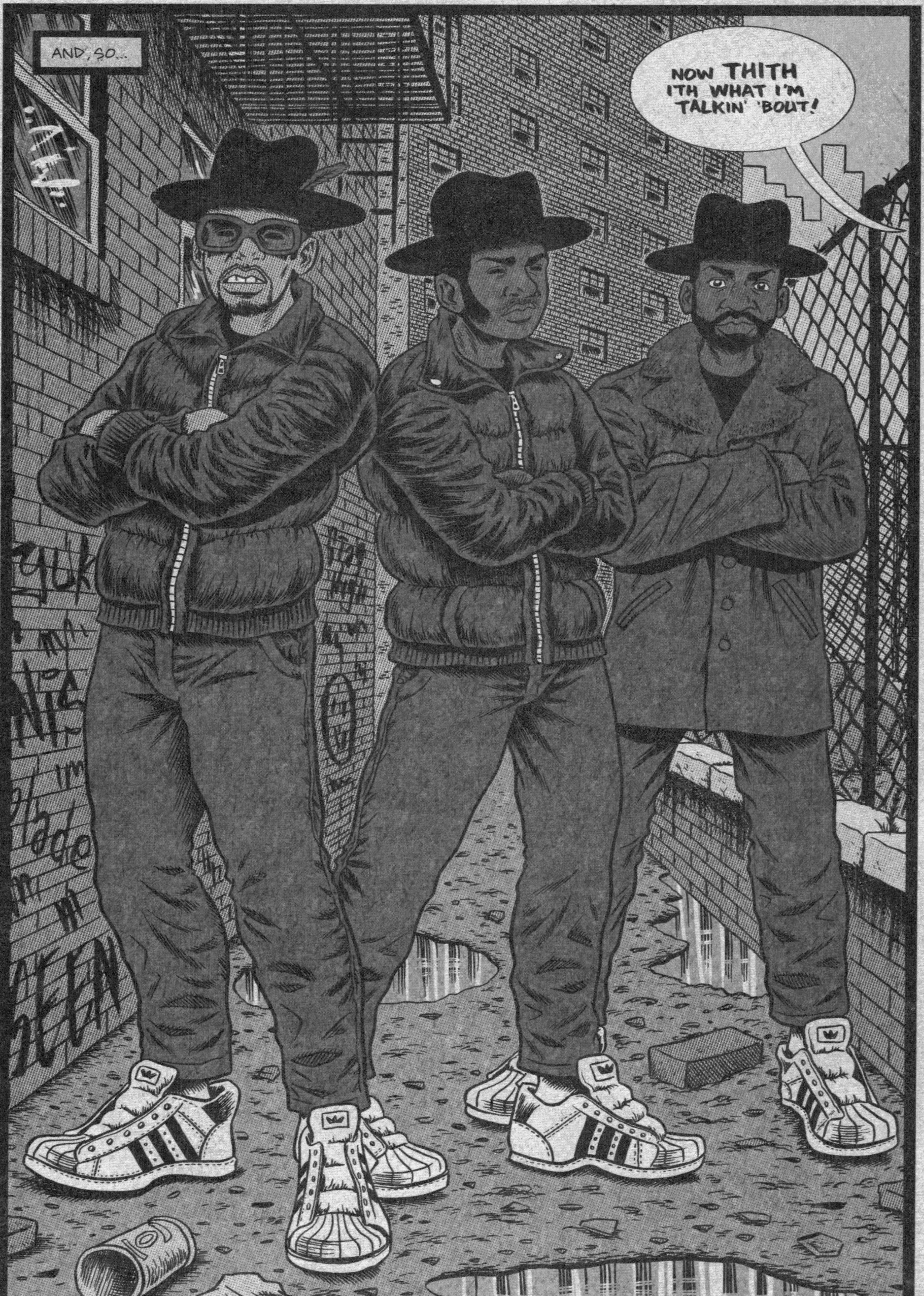
AND, SO...
NOW THITH ITH WHAT I'M TALKIN' 'BOUT!

AFTER ADDRESSING SOME EARLY STICKING POINTS, **RUN-DMC** BEGIN GETTING MORE AND MORE COMFORTABLE PERFORMING TOGETHER...

CHECK THIS OUT! 1, 2, **3**, IN THE PLACE TO **BE**, AS IT IS PLAIN TO **SEE**. HE IS **DJ RUN** AN' I AM **DMC**. FUNKY FRESH FOR **1983**...

DJ JAM MASTER JAY, INSIDE THE **PLACE** WITH ALL THE **BASS**, HE LEAVES WITHOUT A **TRACE**, AND HE CAME HERE TONIGHT TO GET ON YOUR **CASE**...

LIVE AT THE FUNHOUSE AUGUST 5, 1983

THEIR RECORD'S **DRASTIC** POPULARITY IN THE STREETS AND ON RADIO NATURALLY PUTS THEM ON THE RADAR OF ENTERPRISING PERFORMERS LOOKING FOR THEIR SHOT. **MR. MAGIC'S** "ENGINEER ALL STAR" **MARLEY MARL** AND HIS RAPPER GIRLFRIEND **DIMPLES D** RECORD A COMPANION TO SUCKER MC'S, AFFECTIONATELY TITLED **SUCKER DJ'S**.

THE SOUND BEHIND SOME UH THE REKKIDS WE PLAY IS SO **WACK!**

THE TRACK IS **ROUGH**, A LITTLE **SCHIZOPHRENIC**, BUT GOOD ENOUGH TO INTEREST MARLEY'S PSEUDO-MENTOR **ARTHUR BAKER**.

MARLEY MARL...

...IS ONE HELLUVA MAN!

BAKER, **VERY GENEROUSLY**, ADVANCES MARLEY **$600** TO RELEASE THE RECORD ON HIS INDY LABEL, **PARTY TIME** RECORDS. THIS FIRST EFFORT DOESN'T MAKE TOO BIG A SPLASH, BUT...

YOU GOT YUH OWN **TR-808**!

YUP. WHENEVER I CATCH A COUPLE EXTRA DOLLARS I'M A KEEP GETTIN' EQUIPMENT. GONNA MAKE A LITTLE **STUDIO** AT THE CRIB.

MARLEY'S COUSIN

MC SHAN

HIP HOP'S **FIRST GENERATION** ISN'T ABOUT TO LET THE CONTENTIOUS LYRICS OF **SUCKER MC'S** GO UNANSWERED. **GRANDMASTER MELLE MEL AND THE FURIOUS FIVE** RECORD THEIR RESPONSE ON A TRACK CALLED **THE TRUTH.**

SCORPIO (AKA MR. NESS)

...ALL MY SONS JUST RUNNIN' THEY MOUTH...

...SO NOW IT'S TIME FOR DADDY TO SPEAK HIS **WORDS!**

KEITH COWBOY

I'VE BEEN ROCKIN' AT PARTIES 8 YEARS OF MY **LIFE.** GOT SHOT WITH A GUN, STABBED WITH A **KNIFE...** *

...HAD TO PAY MY **DUES,** HAD TO LEARN THE **RULES,** HAD TO SEPARATE THE SMART FROM ALL YOU **FOOLS** ...

* SEE HIP HOP FAMILY TREE BOOK #1 -- EBULLIENT ED

GRANDMASTER MELLE MEL

...FROM AROUND THE **WAY,** BACK IN THE **DAY...**

...WE GOT **BEAT** SO YOU COULD GET **PAID** ...

...I AM YOU, BUT YOU AIN'T **ME!**

...BECAUSE YOU DIDN'T START ROCKIN' 'TIL '83!

WITH THAT LINE **MEL** DISCREDITS **DJ RUN'S** WHOLE CAREER IN THE '70S WORKING BEHIND **KURTIS BLOW.** *

* HHFT BOOK 1, ONCE AGAIN.-- EFFERVESCENT ED

MELLE MEL IS THE BEST THAT'LL EVER EXIST...

...AN' IF I GOTTA BE A SUCKA...

...SUCK ON THIS!!

PRINCE AND MICHAEL JACKSON ARE THE DOMINANT PERFORMERS OF THESE EARLY '80S, AND THE WORLD CLASS WRECKIN' CRU WANTS TO CAPTURE THE SAME VIBE BY DOING CUTE DANCE NUMBERS AT EVE AFTER DARK, THEIR NIGHTCLUB JUST OUTSIDE OF COMPTON, CALIFORNIA.

ONE OF THEIR MOST POPULAR ROUTINES IS TO THE TIME'S SONG THE BIRD, WHICH INCLUDES A PIECE AT THE END WHERE LONZO WILLIAMS COMMANDEERS THE MICROPHONE BEFORE DR. DRE AND YELLA FORCE HIM BACKSTAGE.

LONZO WILL OCCASIONALLY HIRE LIVE PROFESSIONAL PERFORMERS TO PLAY THE CLUB IF HE CAN GET THE ACT CHEAP ENOUGH. THIS IS WHY HE'S IN CROSS-COUNTRY CONTACT WITH RUSSELL SIMMONS.

THESE... ARE... THE BREAKS...

RUSS CONVINCES **EVE** TO BRING OUT **RUN-DMC** AT WHAT WILL SHORTLY BECOME AN **EXORBITANT** DISCOUNT.

IT'S LIKE THAT..

THEY DIDN'T QUITE LET LONZO KNOW THAT ALL THEY HAVE IS **10 MINUTES** OF MATERIAL.

WHAT CAN I THAY **LONTHO**? THE BOYTH ONLY HAVE TWO **THONGTH**.

THEETH THIMPLE MUTHA FUCKA'TH BROKE MY LATHT GOOD MIKE, TOO...

THIS 10 MINUTES IS COMPLETELY AND TOTALLY **REVOLUTIONARY** TO **YELLA** AND **DRE**.

RUN-DMC GIVES **LONZO WILLIAMS** A FEW IDEAS AS WELL...

I WANNA MAKE SOME **STREET LEVEL** SHIT LIKE THEM DUDES.

THEY FILLED THE CLUB UP BEKAWTH THEY GOT A POP'LAR REKKID OUT. WE C'N OUTSHINE THEM NEW YAWK THUCKA'TH...

DRE, WE NEED TO GET YOU FITTED FOR THUM THEE-QUIN OUT-FIT'TH. WE NEED TO LOOK REGAL IF WE GONNA MAKE THUM **REKKID'TH**.

N E X T ▷ ROXANNE ROXANNE MAKES A DEF JAM WHILE THE FREAKS COME OUT AT NIGHT!

96

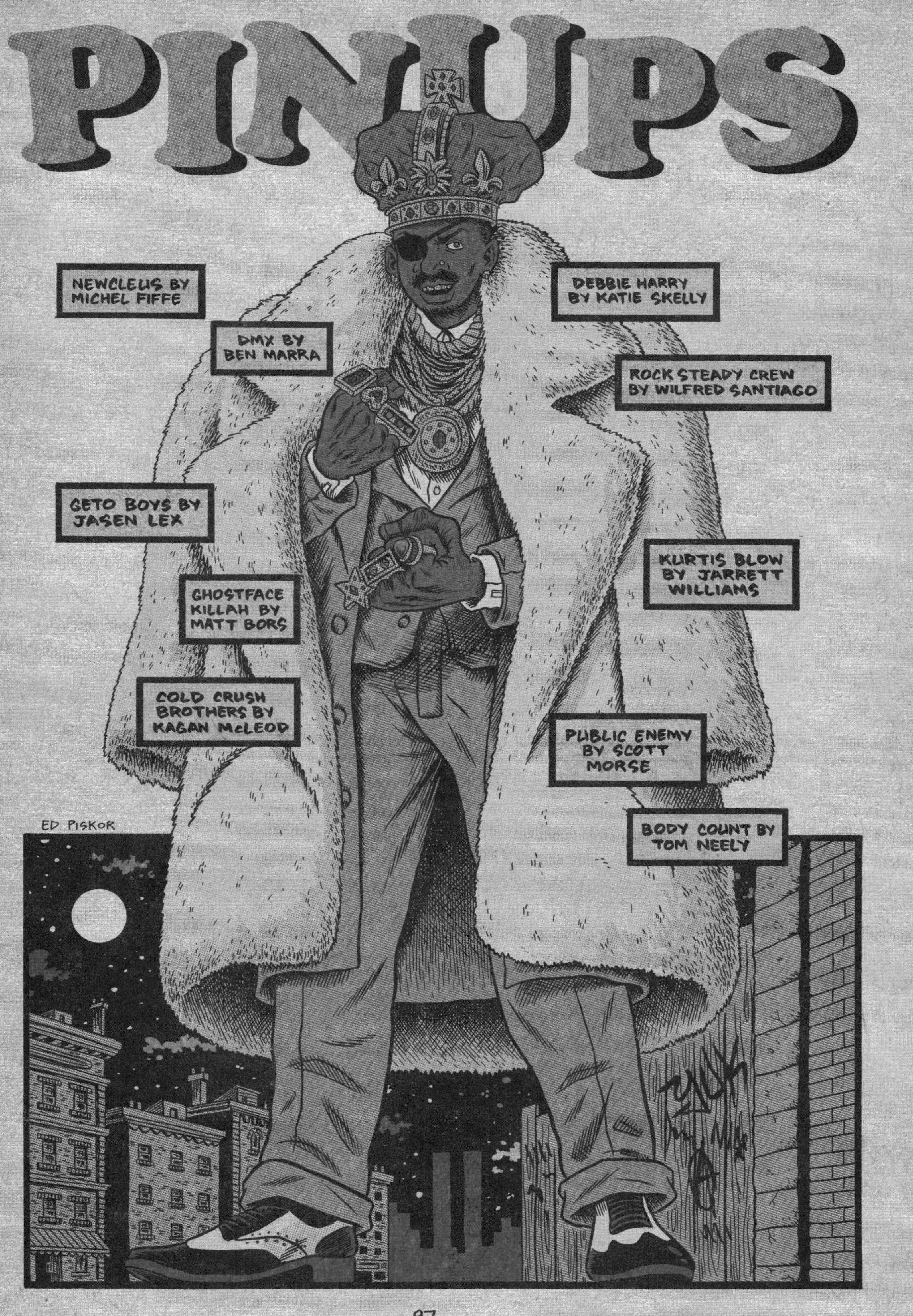
PINUPS
NEWCLEUS BY MICHEL FIFFE
DMX BY BEN MARRA
DEBBIE HARRY BY KATIE SKELLY
ROCK STEADY CREW BY WILFRED SANTIAGO
GETO BOYS BY JASEN LEX
GHOSTFACE KILLAH BY MATT BORS
KURTIS BLOW BY JARRETT WILLIAMS
COLD CRUSH BROTHERS BY KAGAN McLEOD
PUBLIC ENEMY BY SCOTT MORSE
BODY COUNT BY TOM NEELY
ED PISKOR

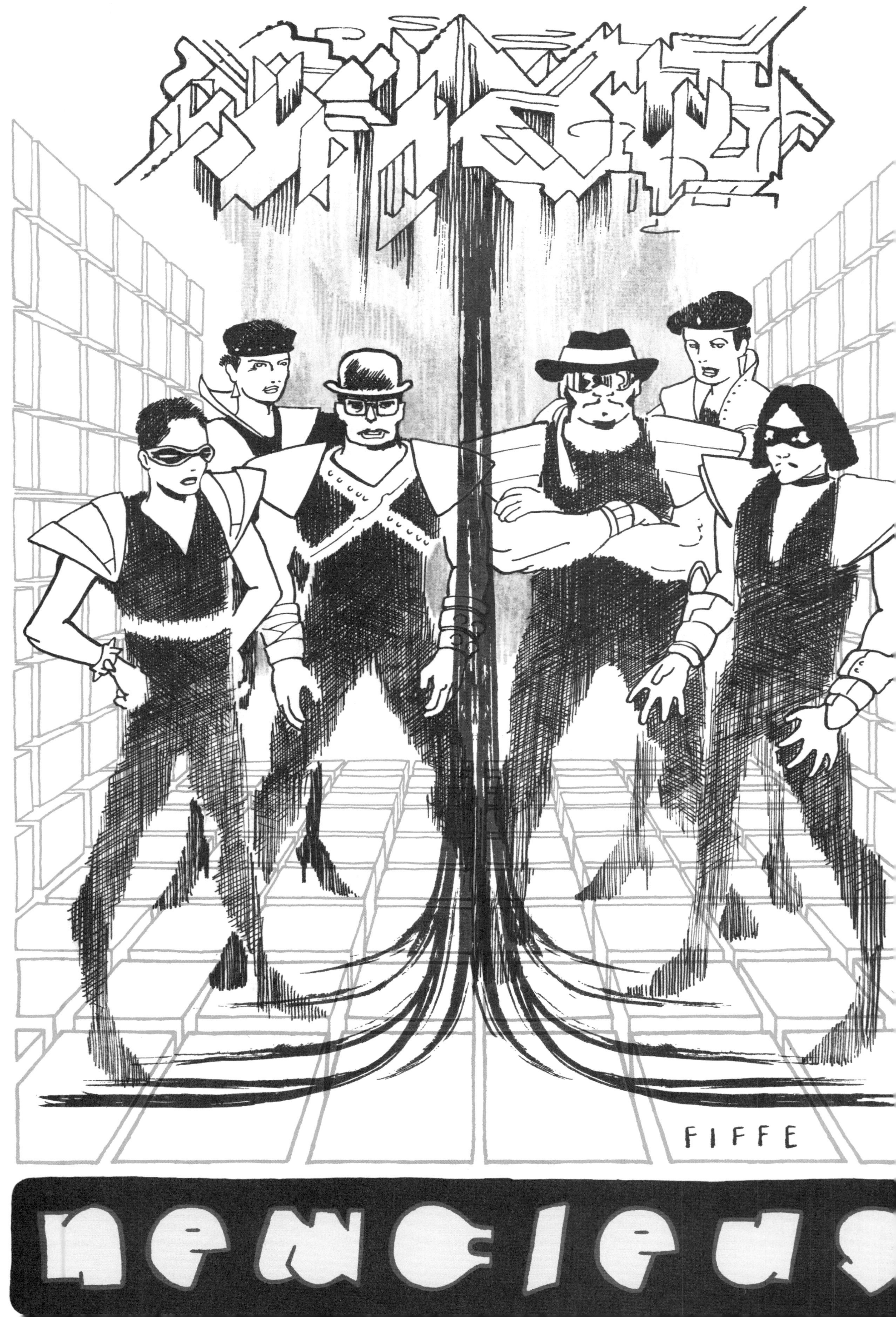
FIFFE
newcleus

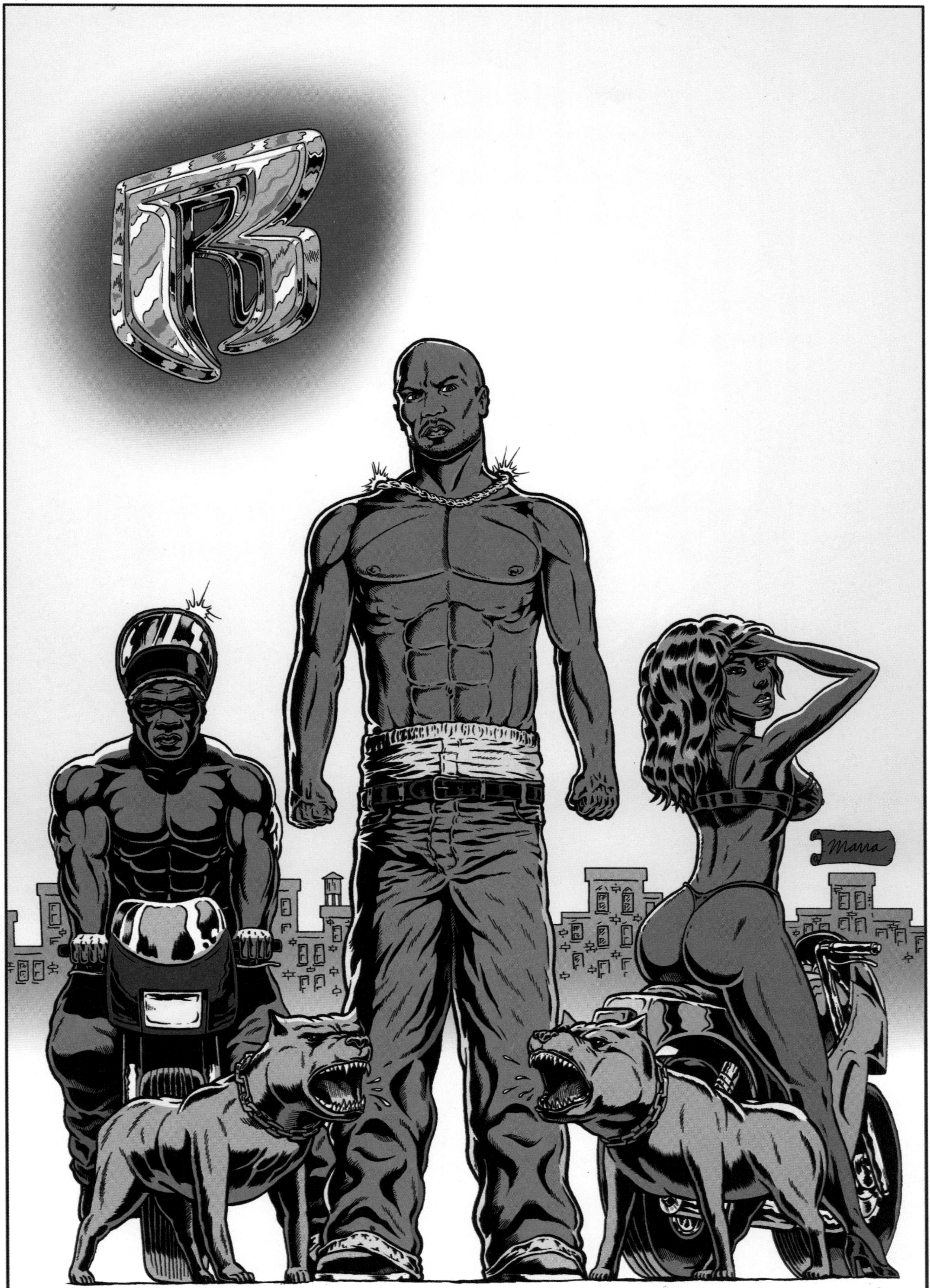
Marra

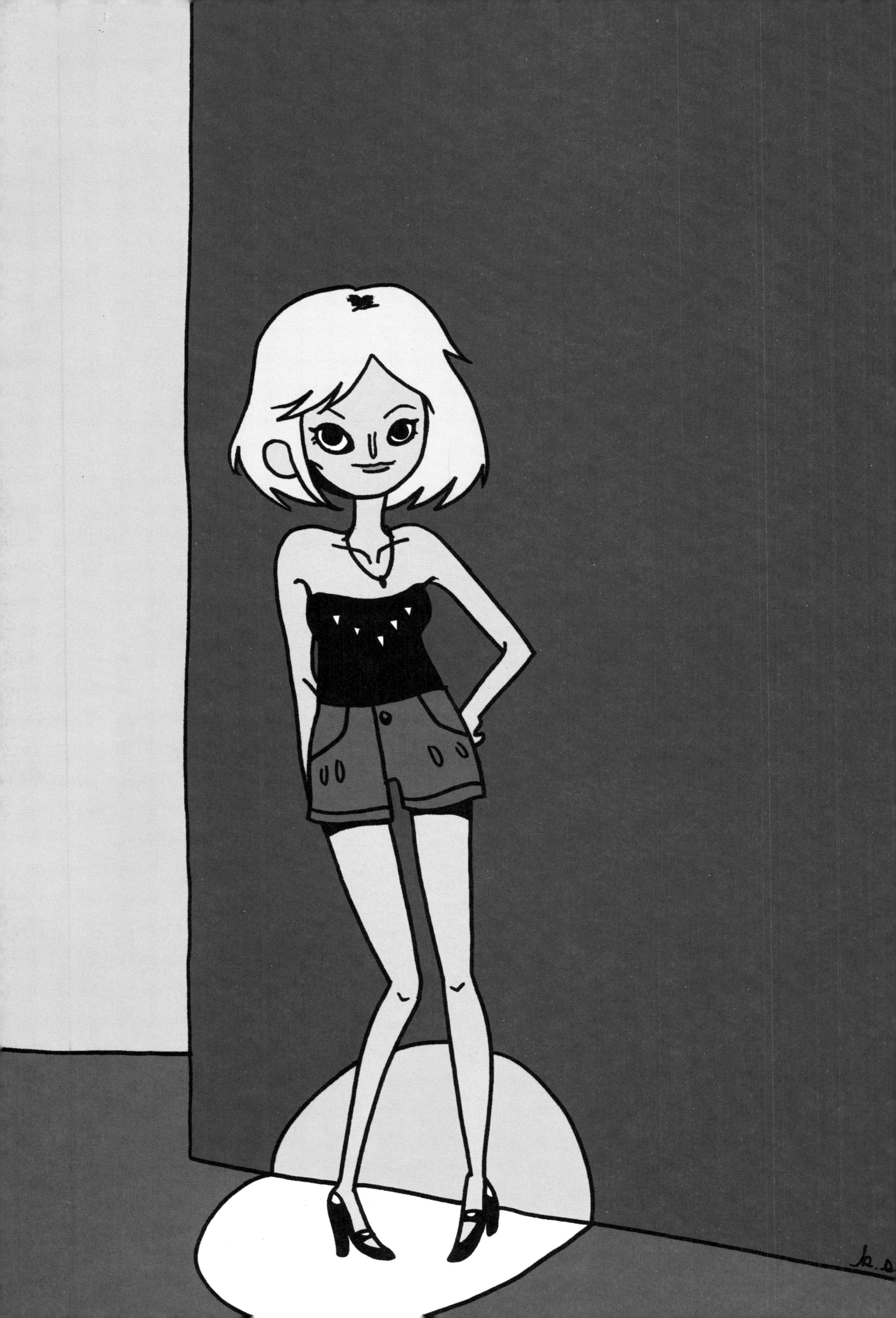

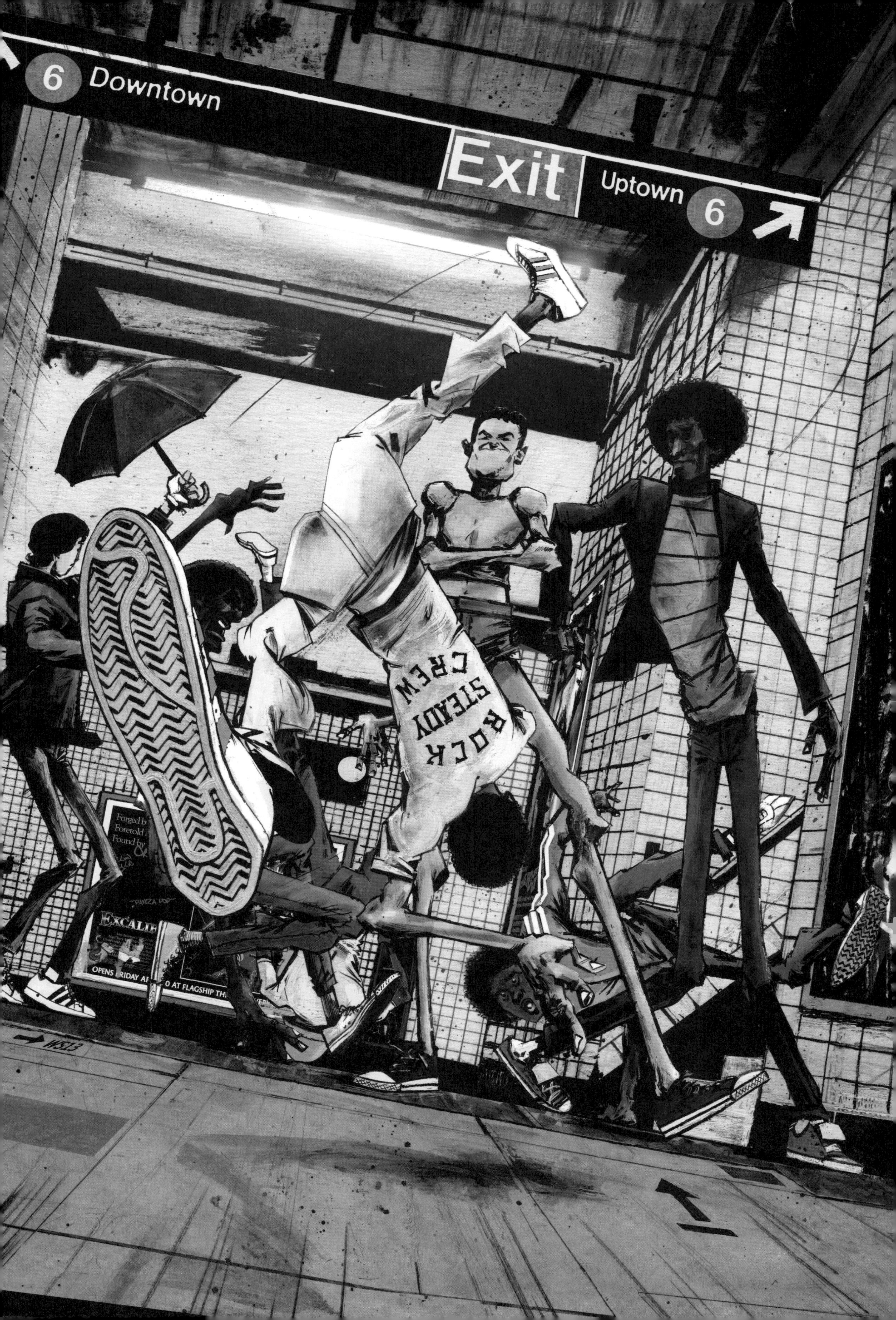
6 Downtown
Exit
Uptown 6
ROCK STEADY CREW

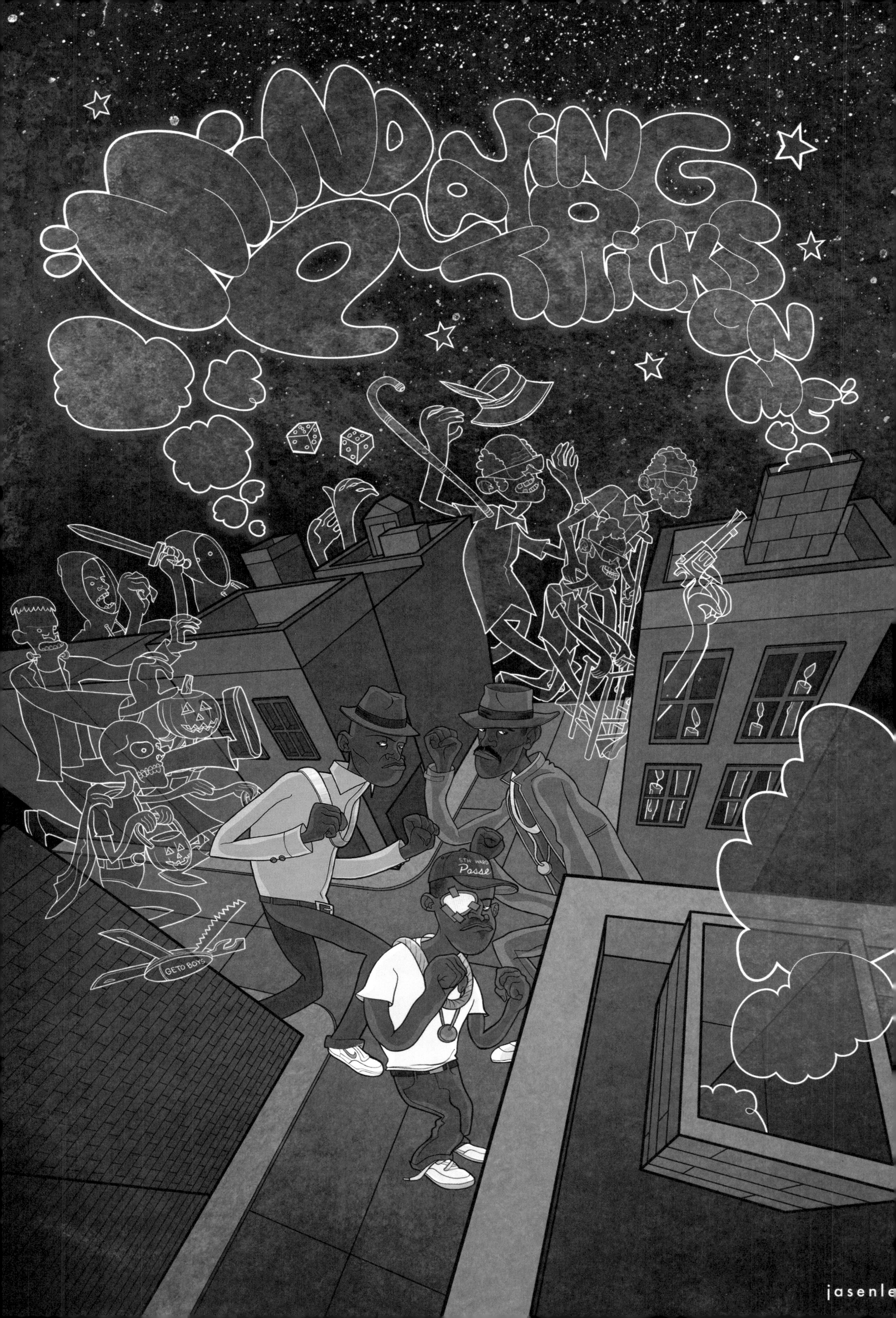

MIND PLAYING TRICKS ON ME
5TH WARD Posse
GETO BOYS
jasenle

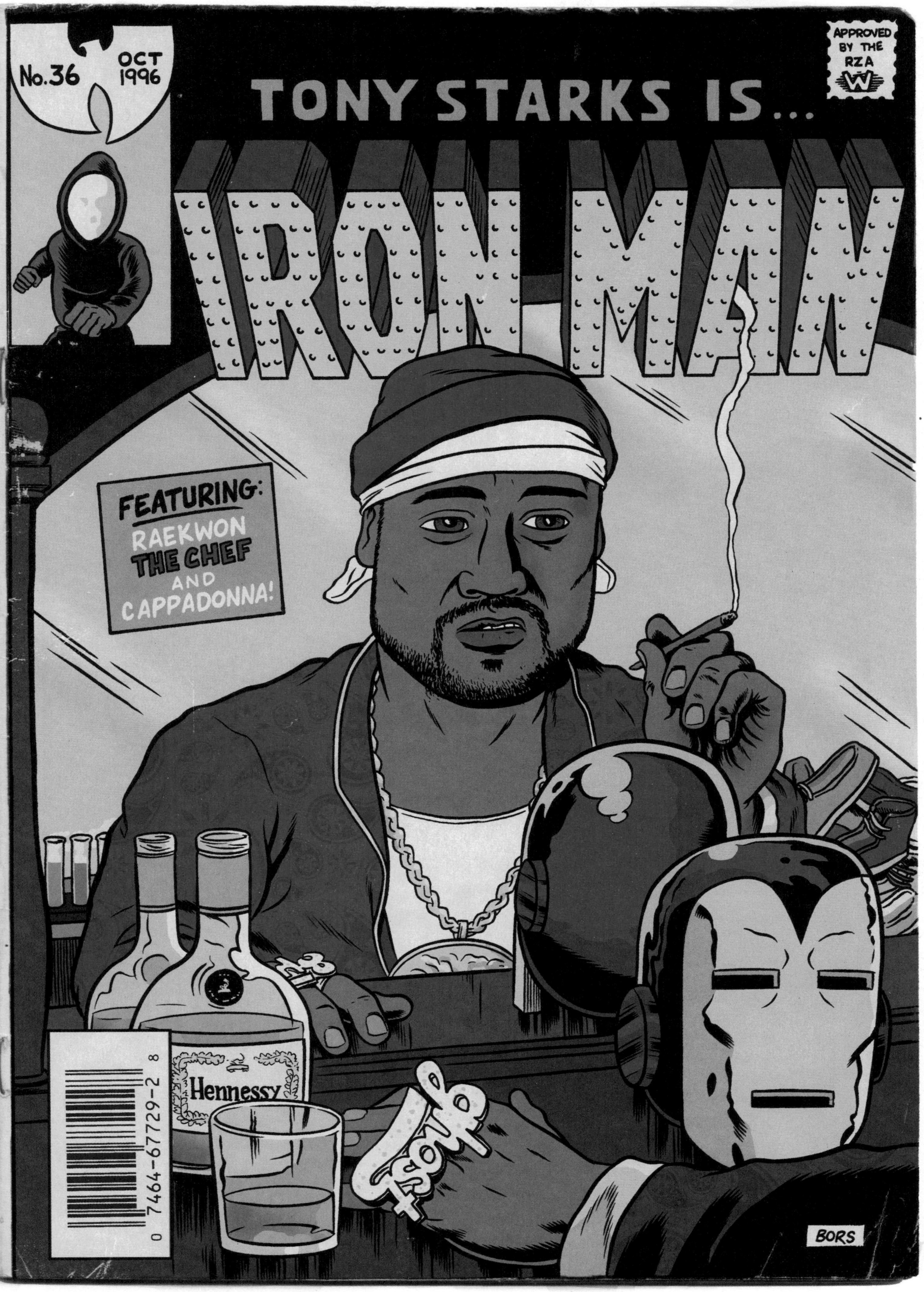
No.36
OCT 1996
APPROVED BY THE RZA
TONY STARKS IS...
IRON MAN
FEATURING: RAEKWON THE CHEF AND CAPPADONNA!
Hennessy
0 7464-67729-2 8
BORS

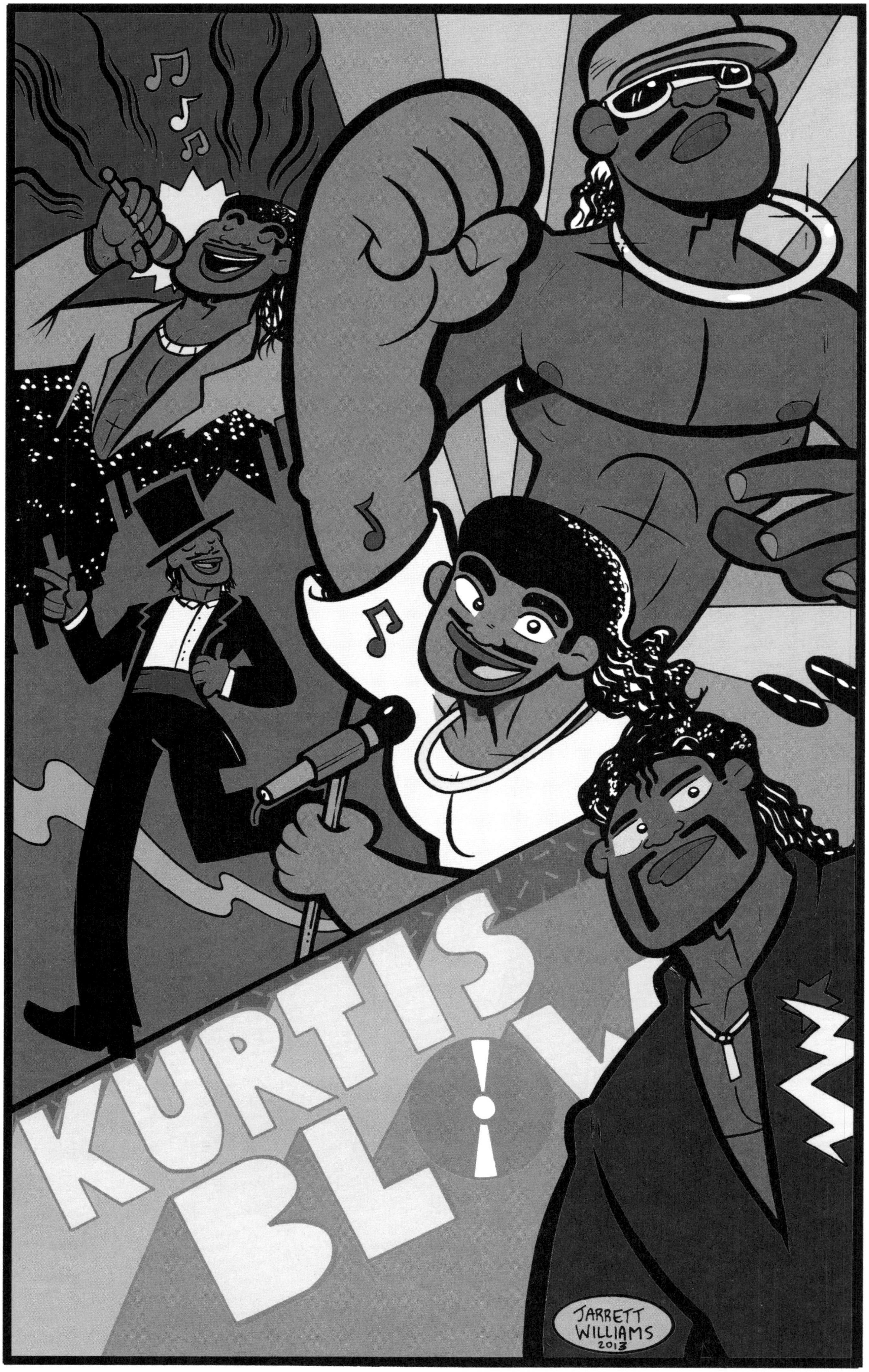
KURTIS BLOW
JARRETT WILLIAMS 2013

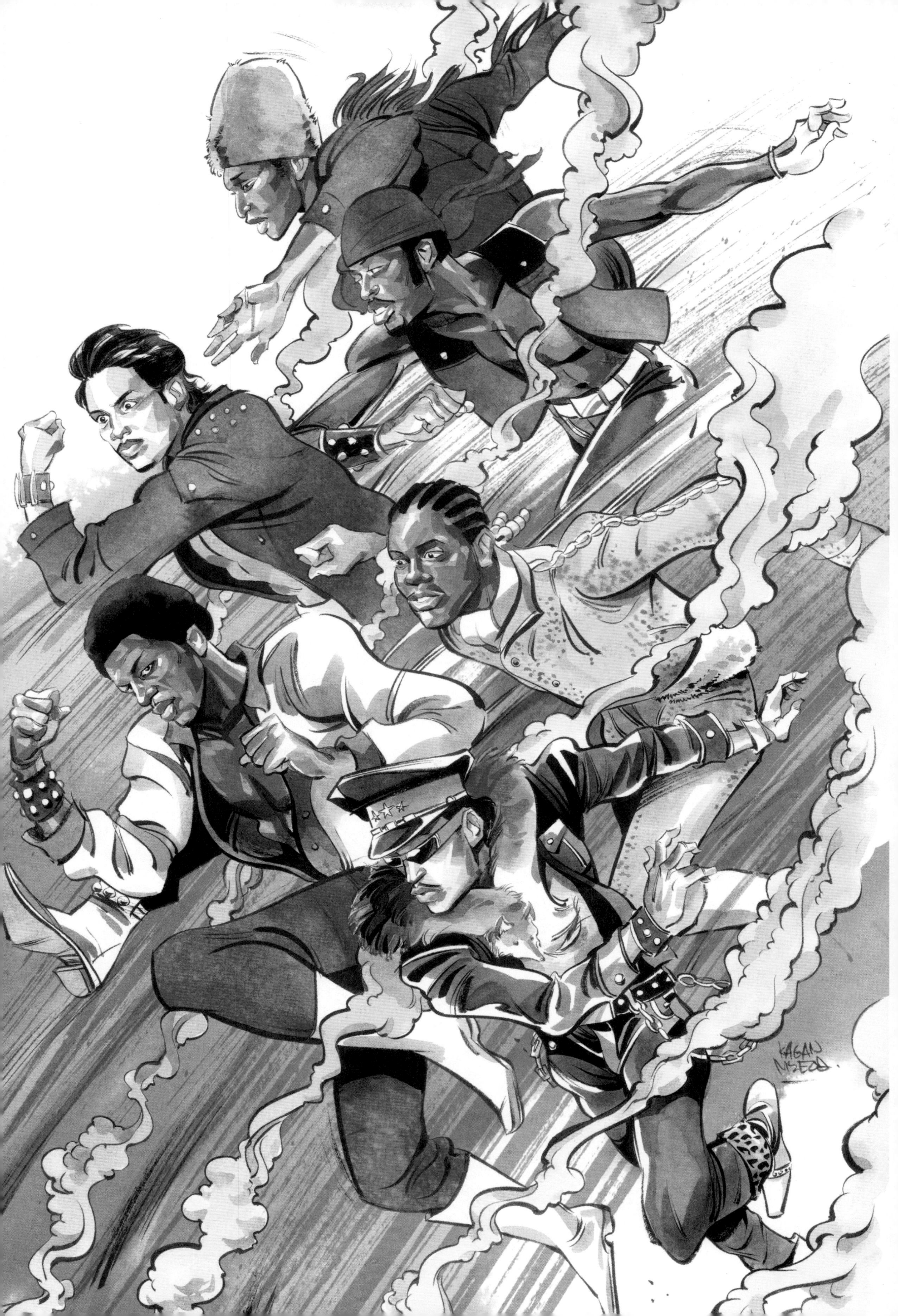
KAGAN

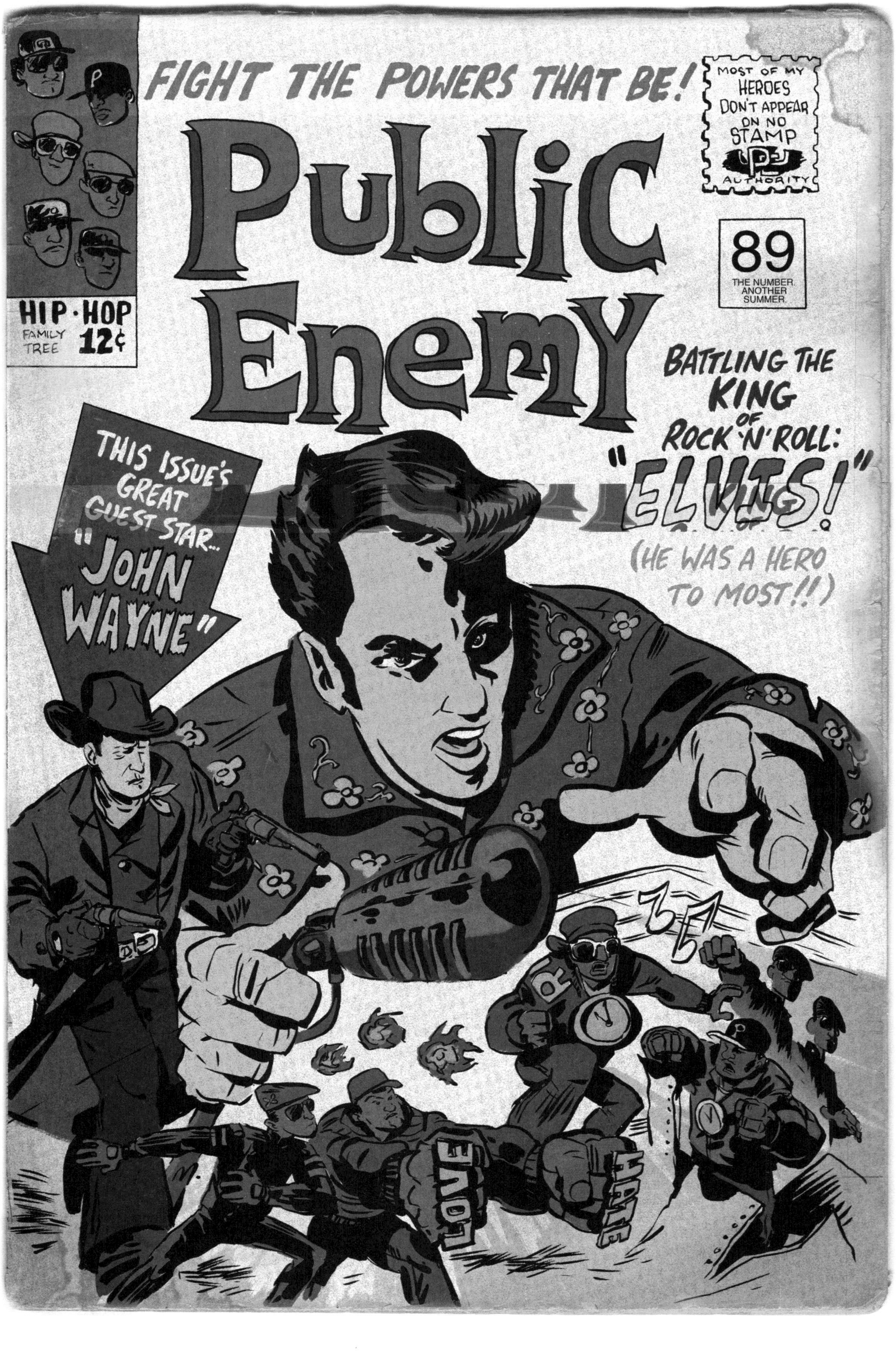
FIGHT THE POWERS THAT BE!
MOST OF MY HEROES DON'T APPEAR ON NO STAMP
AUTHORITY
Public Enemy
HIP·HOP
FAMILY TREE
12¢
89
THE NUMBER. ANOTHER SUMMER.
BATTLING THE KING OF ROCK 'N' ROLL: "ELVIS!"
(HE WAS A HERO TO MOST!!)
THIS ISSUE'S GREAT GUEST STAR... "JOHN WAYNE"
LOVE
HATE

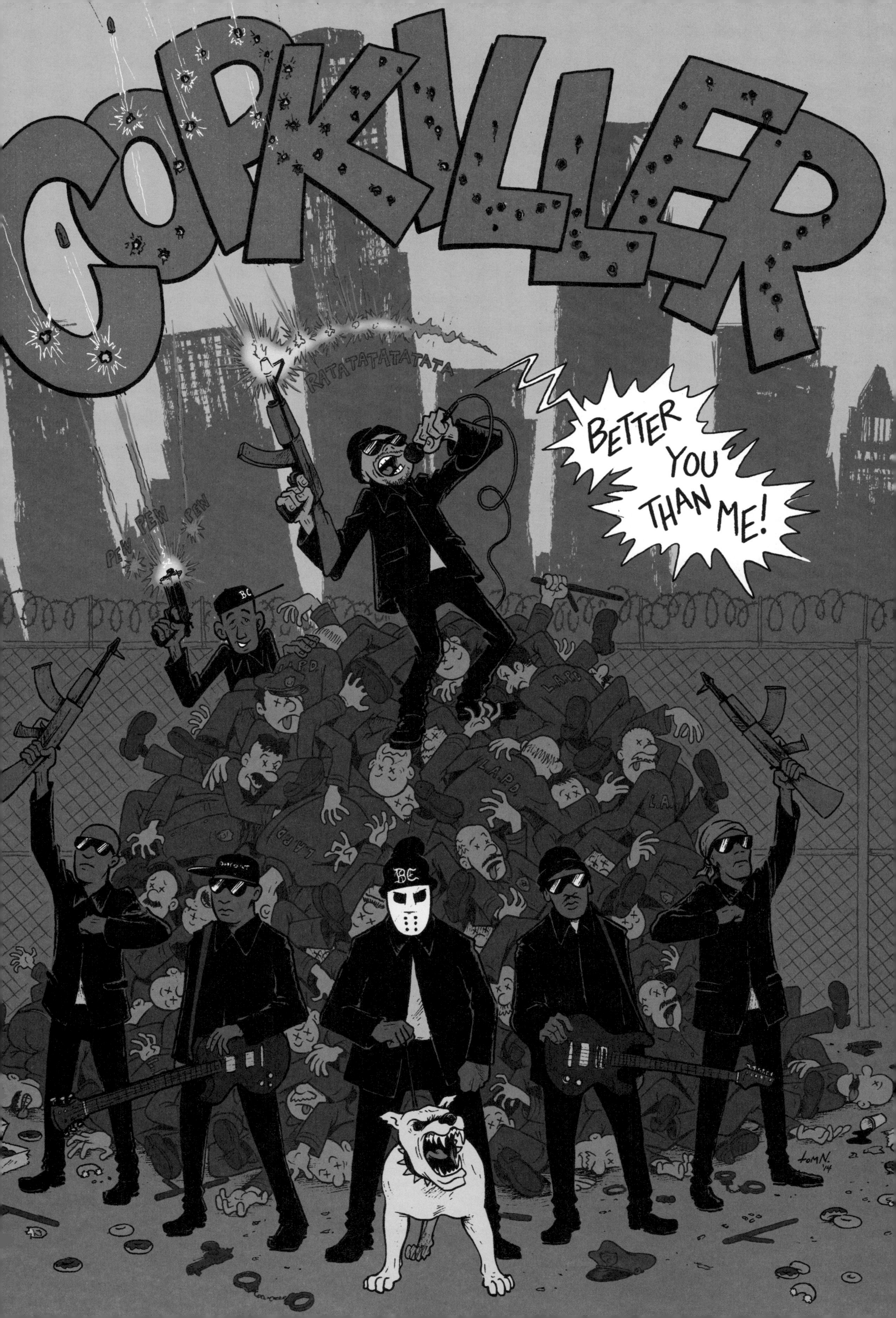
COPKILLER
RATATATATATATATA
BETTER YOU THAN ME!
PEW
PEW
PEW
BC
L.A.P.D.
L.A.P.D.
L.A.P.D.
BC
tomN. '14

BIBLIOGRAPHY

ADLER, BILL. **TOUGHER THAN LEATHER: THE AUTHORIZED BIOGRAPHY OF RUN-DMC**. NEW YORK: NEW AMERICAN LIBRARY, 1987. PRINT.

CHANG, JEFF **CAN'T STOP, WON'T STOP: A HISTORY OF THE HIP-HOP GENERATION**. NEW YORK: ST. MARTIN'S, 2005. PRINT.

CHARNAS, DAN. **THE BIG PAYBACK: THE HISTORY OF THE BUSINESS OF HIP-HOP**. NEW YORK, NY: NEW AMERICAN LIBRARY, 2010. PRINT.

FRESH, FREDDY. **FREDDY FRESH PRESENTS THE RAP RECORDS**. SAINT PAUL, MN: NERBY PUB. LLC, 2004. PRINT.

FRICKE, JIM AND CHARLIE AHEARN. **YES YES Y'ALL: THE EXPERIENCE MUSIC PROJECT ORAL HISTORY OF HIP-HOP'S FIRST DECADE**. CAMBRIDGE, MA: DA CAPO, 2002. PRINT.

ICE-T, AND DOUGLAS CENTURY. **ICE: A MEMOIR OF GANGSTER LIFE AND REDEMPTION-- FROM SOUTH CENTRAL TO HOLLYWOOD**. NEW YORK: ONE WORLD/BALLANTINE, 2011. PRINT.

JENKINS, SACHA. **EGO TRIP'S BOOK OF RAP LISTS**. NEW YORK: ST. MARTIN'S GRIFFIN, 1999. PRINT.

SIMMONS, RUSSELL, AND NELSON GEORGE. **LIFE AND DEF: SEX, DRUGS, MONEY, AND GOD**. NEW YORK, NY: CROWN, 2001. PRINT.

WHISLER, LEAH. **DEF JAM RECORDINGS: THE FIRST 25 YEARS OF THE LAST GREAT RECORD LABEL**. NEW YORK: RIZZOLI, 2011. PRINT.

DISCOGRAPHY

1. **"GENIUS RAP"**: DR. JECKYLL & MR. HYDE (PROFILE)
2. **"IT'S NASTY"**: GRANDMASTER FLASH AND THE FURIOUS FIVE (SUGAR HILL)
3. **"APACHE"** SUGARHILL GANG (SUGAR HILL)
4. **"POSITIVE LIFE"** LOVEBUG STARSKI & THE HARLEM WORLD CREW (TAYSTER)
5. **"A HEARTBEAT RAP"** SWEET G (WEST END)
6. **"CATCH THE BEAT"** T SKI VALLEY (GRAND GROOVE RECORDS)
7. **"CHANGE THE BEAT"** FAB FIVE FREDDY (CELLULOID)
8. **"POLLYWOG STEW EP"** BEASTIE BOYS (RAT CAGE) BOZO MEKO
9. **"FLASH IT TO THE BEAT"** GRANDMASTER FLASH & THE FURIOUS FIVE (SUGAR HILL)
10. **"WEEKEND"** COLD CRUSH BROTHERS (ELITE)
11. **"BUFFALO GALS"** MALCOLM MCLAREN AND THE WORLDS FAMOUS SUPREME TEAM (CHARISMA)
12. **"PLANET ROCK"** AFRIKA BAMBAATAA AND THE SOULSONIC FORCE (TOMMY BOY)
13. **"MAGIC'S WAND"** WHODINI (JIVE)
14. **"SPACE COWBOY"** THE JONZUN CREW (TOMMY BOY)
15. **"CANDY GIRL"** NEW EDITION (STREETWISE)
16. **"ACTION"** ORANGE KRUSH (MERCURY)
17. **"TOUGH"** KURTIS BLOW (MERCURY)
18. **"DAYDREAMIN'"** KURTIS BLOW (MERCURY)
19. **"THE BUBBLE BUNCH"** JIMMY SPICER (MERCURY)
20. **"THE CHALLENGE"** DR. JECKYLL & MR. HYDE (PROFILE)
21. **"WHIP IT"** TREACHEROUS THREE (SUGAR HILL)
22. **"WHIP RAP"** DISCO FOUR (PROFILE)
23. **"COUNTRY ROCK AND RAP"** DISCO FOUR (ENJOY)
24. **"YES WE CAN-CAN"** TREACHEROUS THREE (SUGAR HILL)
25. **"THE MESSAGE"** GRANDMASTER FLASH AND THE FURIOUS FIVE (SUGAR HILL)
26. **"COLD WIND-MADNESS/THE COLDEST RAP"** ICE-T (SATURN)
27. **"MESSAGE II (SURVIVAL)"** MELLE MEL AND DUKE BOOTEE (SUGAR HILL)
28. **"SCORPIO"** GRANDMASTER FLASH AND THE FURIOUS FIVE (SUGAR HILL)
29. **"NEW YORK NEW YORK"** GRANDMASTER FLASH & THE FURIOUS FIVE (SUGAR HILL)
30. **"ACTION"** TREACHEROUS THREE (SUGAR HILL)
31. **"SPOONIE IS BACK"** SPOONIE GEE (SUGAR HILL)
32. **"MAKING CASH MONEY"** BUSY BEE (SUGAR HILL)
33. **"CHECK IT OUT"** WAYNE & CHARLIE (SUGAR HILL)
34. **"GRANDMIXER CUTS IT UP"** GRANDMIXER DST AND THE INFINITY RAPPERS (CELLULOID)
35. **"TOUCH THE ROCK"** COUNT COOLOUT (BOSS)
36. **"I BELIEVE IN THE WHEEL OF FORTUNE"** TANYA & PAULETTE WINLEY (PAUL WINLEY)
37. **"ROCKIN' IT"** FEARLESS FOUR (ENJOY)
38. **"COOKY PUSS"** BEASTIE BOYS (RAT CAGE)
40. **"GETTING OVER"** KOOL KYLE THE STAR-CHILD (FRILLS)
41. **"BEAT BOP"** RAMMELLZEE VS. K-ROB (TARTOWN)
42. **"LOOKING FOR THE PERFECT BEAT"** AFRIKA BAMBAATAA AND THE SOULSONIC FORCE (TOMMY BOY)
43. **"RENEGADES OF FUNK"** AFRIKA BAMBAATAA AND THE SOULSONIC FORCE (TOMMY BOY)
44. **"MALCOLM X (NO SELL OUT)"** KEITH LEBLANC (TOMMY BOY)
45. **"WHITE LINES"** GRANDMASTER AND MELLE MEL (SUGAR HILL)
46. **"PLAY THE BEAT MR. DJ"** G.L.O.B.E AND WHIZ KID (TOMMY BOY)
47. **"LESSON 1 (PAYOFF MIX)"** DOUBLE DEE & STEINSKI (AN EASY TO FIND BOOTLEG)
48. **"ROCKIT"** HERBIE HANCOCK (COLUMBIA
49. **"IT'S LIKE THAT/SUCKER MC'S"** RUN-DMC (PROFILE)

FUNKY INDEX

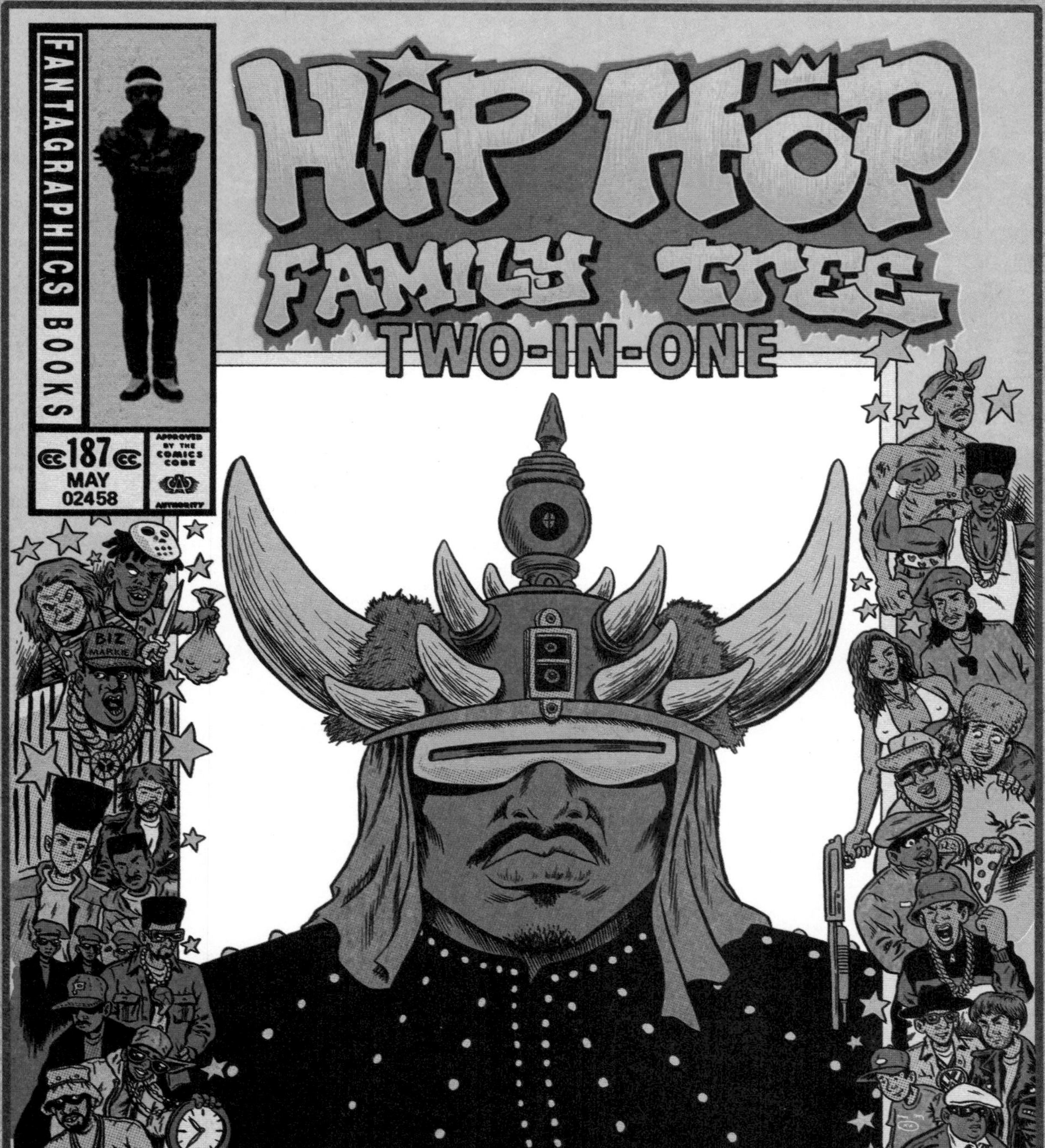
FANTAGRAPHICS BOOKS
HIP HOP FAMILY TREE
TWO-IN-ONE
187
MAY
02458
APPROVED BY THE COMICS CODE AUTHORITY
ED PISKOR

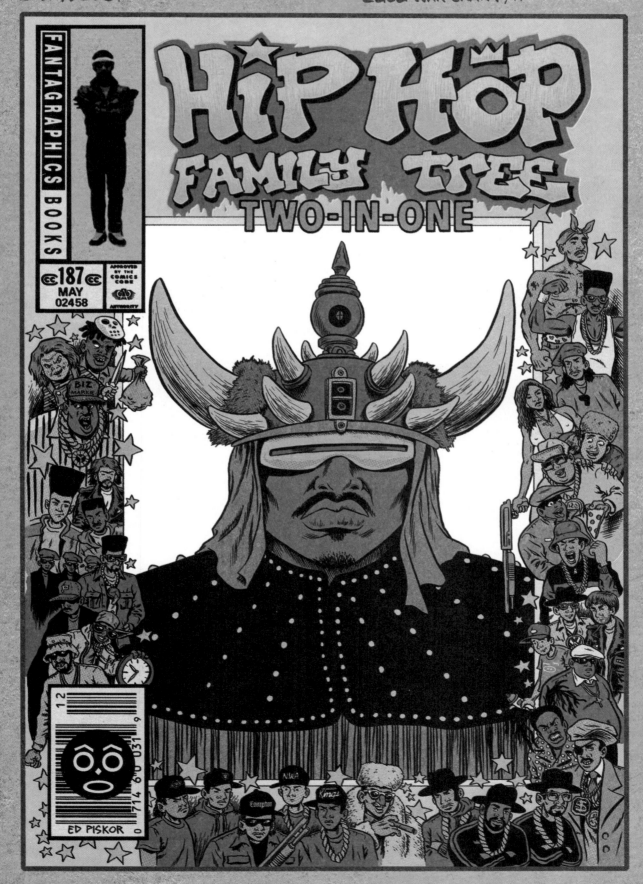

ED PISKOR ED PISKOR **ED PISKOR** ED PISKOR ED PISKO
P HOP FAMILY TREE HIP HOP FAMILY TREE HIP HOP FAM
D PISKOR ED PISKOR ED PISKOR ED PISKOR ED PISKO
P HOP FAMILY TREE HIP HOP **HIP HOP** FAMILY TREE HIP HOP FAM
D PISKOR ED PISKOR ED PISKOR ED PISKOR ED PISKO
P HOP FAMILY TREE HIP HOP **FAMILY TREE** HIP HOP FAM

ED PISKOR, HOMESTEAD, PA (1982–_____)
FILL IN THE BLANK

ED CUT HIS TEETH DRAWING **AMERICAN SPLENDOR** COMICS FOR **HARVEY PEKAR**. THE DUO DID 2 GRAPHIC NOVELS TOGETHER, **MACEDONIA** (2007, VILLARD) AND **THE BEATS** (2009, HILL & WANG). HE DESIGNED ALL THE CHARACTERS FOR A WHOLE SERIES OF **ADULT SWIM** CARTOONS THAT AIRED AT 12:30 ON SUNDAYS. **WIZZYWIG** (2012, TOP SHELF) CAME NEXT AND NOW THERE'S THIS SERIES YOU ARE HOLDING IN YOUR HAND, UPDATED WEEKLY THANKS TO THE HAPPY MUTANTS OVER AT **BOINGBOING.NET**.

PISKOR FEELS LIKE HE CRACKED THE CODE BY CREATING **HIP HOP FAMILY TREE** BECAUSE EVERY SECOND OF MAKING THE COMIC IS EXCITING, EDUCATIONAL, AND DEEPLY ENGAGING.

IN FACT, HE MAY PROBABLY BE DRAWING FRESH STRIPS AS YOU READ THIS. EMAIL HIM AT **WIMPYRUTHERFORD@GMAIL.COM** AND RE-MIND HIM TO EAT SOMETHING. HE POSTS EPHEMERA ROUTINELY ON TWITTER **@EDPISKOR**, SAME GOES FOR TUMBLR.

HIS WEBSITE IS **EDPISKOR.COM** AND IT IS POSSIBLE TO BUY ART FROM THE BOOK. YOU JUST GOTTA ASK.